Ladies' Home Journal

Easy as 1-2-3

COOKBOOK LIBRARY

Ladies' Home Journal

Easy as 1-2-3

NUTRITIOUS & DELICIOUS COOKBOOK

by the Editors of Ladies' Home Journal

PUBLISHED BY LADIES' HOME JOURNAL BOOKS

Ladies' Home Journal

Myrna Blyth, Editor-in-Chief
Sue B. Huffman, Food Editor
Jan T. Hazard, Associate Food Editor
Tamara Schneider, Art Director

Produced in association with Media Projects Incorporated

Carter Smith, Executive Editor
Ellen Coffey, Senior Project Editor
Donna Ryan, Project Editor
Bernard Schleifer, Design Consultant
Design by Bruce Glassman

Preface

*Do you remember a time when people didn't talk about dieting?
Or maybe you can still recall when they didn't discuss over the
dinner table the newest findings about salt or cholesterol. Or
when fiber was more associated with what you were wearing
than with what you were eating.*

*Well, those days are gone forever. Doctors now know that
diet is a significant factor in the development of heart disease,
cancer, diabetes and osteoporosis. Because of this new realization
of the relationship between nutrition and health, many of us have
changed the way we eat.*

In preparing this Easy as 1-2-3 Nutritious & Delicious
Cookbook *at Ladies' Home Journal, we've been very aware of
two of women's highest priorities: saving time in the kitchen and
yet serving their families meals that are good for them. We think
you'll find that the recipes in this book achieve both these goals.
Whether the following menus are low in fat, high in fiber, low in
calories or high in calcium, they can be prepared in thirty minutes
or less, and they are filled with recipes that are absolutely delicious, quick to make and just as quick to garner compliments. We
think you'll find that this unique cookbook is perfect for today's
busy, healthy lifestyle.*

Myrna Blyth

Editor-in-Chief
Ladies' Home Journal

Contents

Fish with Vitamin-Rich Vegetables and Fruit 30
Baked Salmon Steaks with Grated Onion and Worcestershire Sauce, Broccoli with Mock Hollandaise Sauce, Chicory and Romaine Salad, Strawberry Whip

Oven-Poached Fish Rolls 36
Dilled Fillets of Sole Amandine, Steamed New Potatoes, Green Beans with Pimiento, Fruit-Topped Pound Cake

Classic Main Dish with a Chilled Soup 40
Carrot Vichyssoise, Chef's Salad, Rye Rolls with Caraway Seed, Banana Cupcakes

Chicken Cutlets with Coriander and Lime 42
Lime Broiled Breast of Chicken, Orange Rice, Brocoli Florets with Toasted Almonds, Fresh Fruit in Mint

Turkey with Fragrant Spices 44
Spicy Turkey Cutlets, Couscous or Rice, Minted Green Peas, Cinnamon Walnut Sundaes

Refreshing and Unusual Springtime Pasta 46
Fettuccine with Papaya and Asparagus, Cherry Tomatoes and Sugar Snap Peas, Berries with Cannoli Cream

Broiled Fish with Horseradish and Tomato 48
Swordfish Diablo, New Potatoes with Chopped Parsley, Fresh Spinach with Green Onions, Poached Oranges

Zesty Quick-Cooking Cutlets 52
Turkey Piccata, Carrots with Chopped Parsley, Green Salad with Low-Calorie Dressing, Fruit Medley

Protein-Packed Indian Curry 56
Bombay Curry with Rice, Raita, Chutney, Fruit Parfaits

Chicken with Oriental Vegetables 56
Chicken Stir-Fry, Marinated Cucumbers and Onions, Rice, Pineapple Strawberry Boats

Beef Casserole with Mozzarella Cheese 58
La Strata, Tossed Green Salad, Whole Wheat French Bread, Whole Earth Sundaes

Turkey Breast with Vegetables 62
Turkey Vegetable Platter, Whole Wheat Rolls, Black Beauty Sundaes

Fish Fillets with Fresh Asparagus 66
Fish Salad Verde, Natural Asaparagus, Whole Wheat Crisps, Orange Ice

Seafood Salad with Homemade Melba Toast 68
Shrimp with Avocado, Marinated Sliced Tomatoes, Melba Toast with Dill, Berry Sherbet or Ice

Introduction

Isn't it terrific that today eating healthily is eating well and vice-versa? We've come a long way since low-calorie meant grapefruit and cottage cheese and nutritious meant wheat germ and black-strap molasses.

In our Ladies' Home Journal Easy as 1-2-3 Nutritious & Delicious Cookbook *we offer thirty-six menus to complement your fitness-aware, constantly busy lifestyle. Everybody we know is eating more fish. If you're not, you should be. Cooking fish is a snap, and we make it super-easy with such soul-satisfying recipes as Dilled Fillets of Sole Amandine, Gingered Halibut and Swordfish Diablo. There is even a Fish Salade Verde with fresh spinach and a lime-yogurt dressing.*

There are some innovative dishes to add to your culinary repertoire: Fettucine with Papaya and Asparagus, and Spinach Tofu Stir-Fry. (Don't knock tofu if you haven't tried it. It's high in protein, low in fat and calories and very versatile.) There are some variations on familiar themes, such as Turkeyburgers and Chicken Piquante, all contained in nutritionally balanced menus —menus that fill you up without, so to speak, filling you out.

Nutritious & Delicious gives you interesting side-dish ideas as well: Broccoli with Mock Hollandaise, Gingered Lentils, Artichokes Provençal. And the end of your meal can be just as tasty and nutritious as the start, with desserts like Berries with Cannoli Cream, Strawberry-Rhubarb Fool and Poached Pears.

With this new cookbook in your kitchen, "good for you" can mean truly delicious as well.

Sue B. Huffman

Food Editor
Ladies' Home Journal

Gingered Halibut Steaks

TARRAGON, GINGER AND LEEK ADD ZEST

This low-fat halibut entree will be a welcome addition to your collection of fish recipes. The springtime rhubarb dessert is rich in fiber but low in calories.

Menu for 4

- **Gingered Halibut Steaks Steamed Cauliflower**
- **Nutty Brussels Sprouts**
- **Strawberry-Rhubarb Fool**

SHOPPING LIST

- ☐ 4   halibut steaks (1½ pounds), cut about 1 inch thick
- ☐ 1   leek
- ☐ 1   10-ounce container Brussels sprouts
- ☐ 1   pound carrots
- ☐ 1   head cauliflower
- ☐ ½   pint strawberries
- ☐ 1   lemon
- ☐ 1   piece fresh ginger root
- ☐ 1   small can or package chopped walnuts
- ☐ 1   small package quick-cooking tapioca
- ☐ 1   20-ounce package frozen rhubarb or ⅔ pound fresh rhubarb

Have on Hand

- ☐   Sugar
- ☐   Salt
- ☐   Eggs
- ☐   Margarine
- ☐   Orange juice
- ☐   Cinnamon
- ☐   Tarragon

SCHEDULE

1. Prepare Strawberry-Rhubarb Fool.
2. Steam cauliflower.
3. Prepare Nutty Brussels Sprouts.
4. Cook Steamed Halibut Steaks.

Gingered Halibut

1   *leek, thinly sliced*
1   *tablespoon grated fresh ginger*
1   *teaspoon tarragon*
4   *halibut steaks (1½ pounds),*
     cut about 1 inch thick
1   *lemon, quartered*

In small bowl combine leek, ginger and tarragon. Grease a large heatproof plate; scatter on half the seasoned leeks. Lay halibut steaks on top. Sprinkle remaining leek mixture over halibut.

Into large saucepot or Dutch oven pour 1 inch water; set round steamer rack in water. Place plate with halibut on top of rack; cover pan tightly. Steam over medium-high heat 7 to 10 minutes, until fish turns opaque. (Water should boil gently during steaming.) Serve with lemon wedges.

Nutty Brussels Sprouts

1   *container (10 oz.) fresh*
     Brussels sprouts, trimmed
½   *cup diagonally-sliced carrots*
1   *tablespoon margarine*
1   *teaspoon sugar*
¼   *cup chopped walnuts*
⅛   *teaspoon salt*
     Dash cinnamon

In saucepan bring 1 inch water to a boil. Place steamer rack or metal colander in saucepan and add sprouts and carrots. Cover and steam 6 to 8 minutes.

In medium skillet melt margarine; add sugar and stir until dissolved. Add walnuts and cook, stirring frequently, until browned. Stir in sprouts, carrots, salt and cinnamon; toss until well coated.

Strawberry-Rhubarb Fool

½   *package (20 oz.) frozen*
     cut rhubarb or 2½ cups
     fresh rhubarb, cut into
     1-inch slices
1   *cup sliced strawberries*
½   *cup orange juice*
1½   *tablespoons quick-cooking*
     tapioca
¼   *cup sugar, divided*
1   *egg white*

In large saucepan combine rhubarb, strawberries, orange juice, tapioca and 3 tablespoons sugar; bring to a boil over high heat, stirring occasionally. Remove from heat and refrigerate. In small mixer bowl beat egg white at high speed until soft peaks form. Gradually beat in remaining 1 tablespoon sugar; beat until stiff peaks form. Fold beaten white into rhubarb mixture. Spoon into dessert dishes or stemmed wineglasses.

> # BRUSSELS SPROUTS COMBINATIONS
>
> *For color and good taste, pair them with water chestnuts, wax beans, or baby onions.*

Spinach Tofu Stir-Fry

HIGH-PROTEIN BEAN CURD WITH SPINACH

Tofu provides low-cholesterol, low-fat protein at low cost. Look for it in the produce department of your supermarket or in Oriental food stores.

Menu for 4

- **Hot Tomato Drink**
- **Spinach Tofu Stir-Fry**
- **Cellophane Noodles**
- **Winter Fruit Salad**

SHOPPING LIST

- ☐ 1 pound tofu
- ☐ 1 green pepper
- ☐ 1 bunch celery
- ☐ 2 medium onions
- ☐ 1 large orange
- ☐ 1 medium pear
- ☐ 2 bananas
- ☐ 1 small bunch grapes
- ☐ 1 small package pitted prunes
- ☐ 1 small can or package chopped walnuts
- ☐ 1 32-ounce can or bottle tomato juice
- ☐ 1 package cellophane noodles
- ☐ 1 8-ounce container vanilla yogurt
- ☐ 1 10-ounce package fresh spinach
- ☐ ¼ pound ground beef

Have on Hand
- ☐ Cornstarch

- ☐ Sugar
- ☐ Brown sugar
- ☐ Salt
- ☐ Pepper
- ☐ Garlic
- ☐ Salad oil
- ☐ Cider vinegar
- ☐ Soy sauce
- ☐ Chicken bouillon cubes or granules
- ☐ Horseradish
- ☐ Cinnamon
- ☐ Cardamom or nutmeg
- ☐ Ginger

SCHEDULE

1. Prepare Hot Tomato Drink.
2. Prepare Winter Fruit Salad.
3. Prepare Spinach Tofu Stir-Fry.
4. Cook cellophane noodles.

Hot Tomato Drink

1	quart tomato juice
1	slice onion
1	slice green pepper
1	stalk celery
1/4	cup cider vinegar
1	tablespoon sugar
1	tablespoon horseradish
	Dash pepper

In large saucepan combine all ingredients and heat to boiling. Cover and simmer 20 to 25 minutes; strain.

Spinach Tofu Stir-Fry

1	pound tofu, cut into 1-inch cubes
1/3	cup cornstarch
2	tablespoons salad oil
2	garlic cloves, crushed
1	medium onion, sliced
1/4	pound ground beef
1	package (10 oz.) fresh spinach
1/4	cup water
1	tablespoon brown sugar
3	tablespoons soy sauce
1	tablespoon cider vinegar
1/2	teaspoon ground ginger
1	chicken bouillon cube or 1 teaspoon granules

Drain tofu on paper towels to remove as much liquid as possible. Toss with cornstarch to coat lightly. In large skillet heat oil over medium-high heat. Add tofu and 1 crushed garlic clove; stir-fry until golden. Remove tofu. Add onion, ground beef and remaining garlic; stir-fry until beef loses its pinkness. Add remaining ingredients and simmer 5 minutes. Return tofu to skillet and heat through.

Winter Fruit Salad

1	large orange, cut into chunks
1	medium pear, diced
2	bananas, sliced
1	cup red or purple grapes
1/2	cup diced prunes
1/2	cup chopped walnuts
1	container (8 oz.) low-fat vanilla yogurt
1/4	teaspoon cinnamon
1/8	teaspoon cardamom or nutmeg

In medium bowl combine orange, pear, bananas, grapes, prunes and walnuts; toss well. In small bowl combine yogurt, cinnamon and cardamom or nutmeg until well blended. Add to fruit and toss to coat well. Chill or serve at room temperature.

CARDAMOM TIPS

The fragrant brown seeds of the cardamom add flavor and aroma to many dishes. Use the seeds whole (remove before serving) or buy ground cardamom. If you can obtain whole cardamom pods, try adding 1 or 2 to a batch of fruit punch or a jar of pickles. Use cardamom also to add flavor to:

- *fruit drinks*
- *marinades for veal or chicken*
- *rice*

Fish Fantasia

SOLE OR FLOUNDER FILLETS WITH VEGETABLES

This low-calorie fish entree with tomatoes, onions and green peppers will cook on top of the stove while you prepare the spinach and pasta. Serve sherry-flavored broiled grapefruit for dessert.

Menu for 4

- **Fish Fantasia**
- **Fresh Spinach with Lemon and Mushrooms**

Orzo or Other Tiny Pasta
- **Broiled Grapefruit Halves**

SHOPPING LIST

- ☐ 1½ pounds fresh sole or flounder fillets
- ☐ 1 green pepper
- ☐ 1 pound fresh spinach
- ☐ 1 large or 2 medium onions
- ☐ 2 ounces fresh mushrooms
- ☐ 2 grapefruit
- ☐ 1 lemon
- ☐ 1 16-ounce can tomatoes
- ☐ 1 package orzo or other tiny pasta

Have on Hand

- ☐ Brown sugar
- ☐ Salt
- ☐ Pepper
- ☐ Ground red pepper
- ☐ Margarine
- ☐ Garlic
- ☐ Sherry

SCHEDULE

1. Prepare Fish Fantasia.
2. Cook orzo.
3. Prepare Fresh Spinach with Lemon and Mushrooms.
4. Prepare Broiled Grapefruit Halves.

Fish Fantasia

1½ *pounds sole or flounder*
     fillets
1   *tablespoon margarine*
1   *garlic clove, crushed*
1   *cup sliced onion*
½   *cup diced green pepper*
     Pinch ground red pepper
1   *can (16 oz.) whole*
     tomatoes

Cut fish fillets into chunks. In large heavy skillet melt margarine; add garlic, onion, green pepper and ground red pepper. Cover and cook 5 minutes. Stir in tomatoes; simmer, covered, 5 minutes. Add fish fillets, spoon sauce over fish. Cook, uncovered, 10 minutes.

Fresh Spinach with Lemon and Mushrooms

1   *tablespoon margarine*
½   *cup sliced fresh mushrooms*
1   *teaspoon lemon juice*
1   *pound fresh spinach,*
     thoroughly rinsed,
     stemmed and chopped
¼   *teaspoon salt*
⅛   *teaspoon pepper*
     Lemon wedges

In large skillet melt margarine; add sliced mushrooms and saute 3 minutes. Sprinkle lemon juice over mushrooms. Add spinach to skillet; cover and cook 5 to 7 minutes, stirring occasionally, until spinach is thoroughly wilted. Add salt and pepper. Garnish with lemon wedges.

Broiled Grapefruit Halves

2   *grapefruit*
2   *tablespoons sherry, divided*
¼   *cup brown sugar, divided*

Preheat broiler. Halve and section grapefruit. Sprinkle each half with 1½ teaspoons sherry and 1 tablespoon brown sugar. Broil 2 inches from heat for 3 to 5 minutes or until sugar bubbles. Serve warm.

GRAPEFRUIT TIPS

- *This fruit is a dieter's delight. A medium-size half averages about 65 calories. It is also a dependable source of vitamin C and provides vitamin A, potassium, folic acid and fiber.*
- *Serve grapefruit halves as an appetizer, garnished with fresh strawberries or blueberries, a tablespoon of grenadine or fresh mint leaves.*
- *As a dessert, broiled or chilled, garnish the center with a spoonful of currant jelly or raspberry sherbet.*

Classic Veal Cutlets with Parsley

SAUTEED VEAL WITH ARTICHOKE HEARTS

Serve this simple but delectable veal entree with a salad of fresh, tender lettuce and sweet red peppers. Buy the fragrant flower-flavored water for the dessert in a drugstore or Middle Eastern food shop.

Menu for 4

- **Classic Veal Cutlets with Parsley**
- **Artichokes Provençal**

- **Bibb Lettuce and Red Pepper Salad**
- **Moroccan Orange Slices**

SHOPPING LIST

- ☐ 1½ pounds veal cutlets
- ☐ 2 heads Bibb lettuce
- ☐ 2 red peppers
- ☐ 1 bunch fresh parsley
- ☐ 1 bunch fresh basil or dried basil
- ☐ 4 medium tomatoes
- ☐ 4 small seedless oranges
- ☐ 1 6-ounce can tomato paste
- ☐ 1 small bottle rose or orange-flower water
- ☐ 1 9-ounce package frozen artichoke hearts

Have on Hand
- ☐ Margarine

- ☐ Salt
- ☐ Pepper
- ☐ White pepper
- ☐ Garlic
- ☐ Cinnamon

SCHEDULE

1. Prepare Moroccan Orange Slices.
2. Cook Artichokes Provençal
3. Prepare salad.
4. Prepare Classic Veal Cutlets with Parsley.

Classic Veal Cutlets with Parsley

1½   pounds veal cutlets,
         pounded thin
½   teaspoon salt
⅛   teaspoon white pepper
2   tablespoons margarine
1   garlic clove, crushed
2   tablespoons chopped fresh
         parsley, divided

Season veal on both sides with salt and white pepper to taste. Cut into 2-inch-wide strips. In nonstick skillet brown veal strips 6 to 7 minutes or to desired degree of doneness, stirring occasionally. Transfer to serving platter and keep warm. In small saucepan melt margarine until bubbly. Add garlic and 1 tablespoon parsley; reheat and pour over veal. Garnish with remaining parsley.

Artichokes Provençal

1   package (9 oz.) frozen
         artichoke hearts
4   medium tomatoes, chopped
2   tablespoons tomato paste
2   tablespoons water
2 garlic cloves, finely minced
1   tablespoon chopped fresh
         basil or ½ teaspoon dried
½   teaspoon salt
¼   teaspoon pepper
1   teaspoon chopped parsley

Preheat oven to 375° F. Cook artichoke hearts according to package directions. In small skillet combine tomatoes, tomato paste, water, garlic and basil. Simmer about 5 minutes. Season with salt and pepper. Add parsley. Place artichoke hearts in baking dish and top with sauce. Heat in oven 10 minutes.

Moroccan Orange Slices

4   small seedless oranges,
         peeled
2   to 3 teaspoons rose or
         orange-flower water
      Cinnamon

Cut each orange into 3 equal slices and arrange in 1 layer in serving dish. Sprinkle with flavored water and cinnamon to taste; toss. Cover and marinate until serving time.

HOW TO CHOP FRESH PARSLEY

The secret lies in the chef's, or French, knife and the way you hold it. Use a fairly long-bladed, very sharp knife. Hold the handle firmly in one hand and rest the fingertips of your other hand on the top of the knife blade. Guide the knife rapidly in a seesaw fashion as you chop or mince each clump of parsley. Slice with even strokes until chopped to desired fineness. Keep scraping chopped parsley into a pile and out of your way.

Spinach Linguine with Spring Sauce

HIGH-FIBER MEATLESS PASTA MENU

Crisp vegetables add texture and color to this vitamin-packed entree. A generous sprinkling of Parmesan cheese provides calcium as well as flavor. The creamy peach dessert is made with low-fat ricotta cheese and nutrient-rich wheat germ.

Menu for 4

- **Spinach Linguine with Spring Sauce Asparagus**

- **Sliced Peaches with Ricotta Cream**

SHOPPING LIST

- ☐ 1   8-ounce package spinach linguine
- ☐ 1½   pounds fresh asparagus
- ☐ 1   large onion
- ☐ 1   medium zucchini
- ☐ 1   pound carrots
- ☐ 4   large ripe peaches
- ☐ 1   bunch fresh basil or dried basil
- ☐ 1   jar wheat germ
- ☐ 1   16-ounce can tomatoes
- ☐ 1   15-ounce container part-skim ricotta cheese

Have on Hand
- ☐   Sugar
- ☐   Salt
- ☐   Parmesan cheese
- ☐   Garlic
- ☐   Olive oil
- ☐   Vanilla extract

SCHEDULE

1. Prepare Spinach Linguine with Spring Sauce.
2. Cook asparagus.
3. Prepare Sliced Peaches with Ricotta Cream.

Spinach Linguine with Spring Sauce

3 tablespoons olive oil
1½ cups diced zucchini
1 cup chopped onion
1 cup diced carrots
1 garlic clove, minced
1 can (16 oz.) tomatoes
1 tablespoon fresh chopped
  basil or ½ teaspoon
  dried
½ teaspoon salt
½ teaspoon sugar
1 package (8 oz.) spinach
  linguine
¾ cup grated Parmesan
  cheese

In large, deep skillet heat oil. Add zucchini, onion, carrots and garlic; cook, stirring occasionally, until vegetables are tender-crisp. Stir in tomatoes and their liquid, basil, salt and sugar. Cover and simmer over low heat 10 to 15 minutes, stirring to break up tomatoes. Cook linguine according to package directions; drain. Add to tomato sauce along with Parmesan. Toss until well coated.

Sliced Peaches with Ricotta Cream

4 large ripe peaches
¼ cup ricotta cheese
2 tablespoons wheat germ

½ teaspoon vanilla extract
  Extra wheat germ for
  garnish

Peel and pit peaches. Slice 3½ peaches into large bowl, reserving ½ peach. In small bowl combine ricotta cheese, wheat germ and vanilla extract. Chop remaining peach half into ricotta mixture; stir to mix. Spoon sliced peaches into 4 dessert dishes and top each dish with a rounded tablespoon ricotta mixture. Sprinkle with additional wheat germ.

QUICK CRUNCH WITH WHEAT GERM

- Add ¼ cup wheat germ to ground meat before cooking.
- Top fish with almonds, lemon juice and wheat germ before broiling.
- Sprinkle on top of baked apples, pears, peaches.
- Before oven-frying chicken, dredge in mixture of wheat germ and flour.
- Roll small cheese balls in wheat germ; top with pecan halves.
- Sprinkle over cooked hot cereals for a little extra nutrition.
- Sprinkle on peanut butter and jelly or cream cheese and jelly sandwiches before closing them.

Vegetable Burgers

BURGERS AND VEGETABLES THE EASY WAY

Put your food processor to work in preparing these vegetable-packed hamburgers. Then cook them in the broiler along with the herbed zucchini. Add pita bread for the last few minutes, until toasted the way you like it. The result? A simple but tasty and nourishing meal.

Menu for 4

- **Vegetable Burgers Toasted Pita Breads**
- **Zucchini with Basil**
- **Strawberries with Kirsch**

SHOPPING LIST

- ☐ 2 carrots
- ☐ 1 bunch celery
- ☐ 1 small onion
- ☐ 1 pound zucchini
- ☐ 1 pint fresh strawberries
- ☐ 1 bunch fresh basil or dried basil
- ☐ 1 small can or package shredded coconut
- ☐ 1 small jar wheat germ
- ☐ 4 pita breads
- ☐ 1 pound ground beef

Have on Hand
- ☐ Salt
- ☐ Pepper
- ☐ Eggs
- ☐ Parmesan cheese
- ☐ Salad oil
- ☐ Worcestershire sauce
- ☐ Kirsch

SCHEDULE

1. Prepare Strawberries with Kirsch.
2. Prepare Vegetable Burgers.
3. Cook Zucchini with Basil.
4. Toast pita breads.

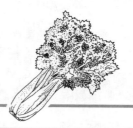

Vegetable Burgers

1   **pound ground beef**
2   **carrots, grated**
2   **ribs celery, chopped**
1   **small onion, chopped**
½   **cup grated Parmesan cheese**
2   **tablespoons Worcestershire sauce**
1   **tablespoon wheat germ**
1   **egg**
½   **teaspoon salt**
¼   **teaspoon pepper**

In large mixing bowl combine all ingredients. Preheat broiler. Form meat into 4 patties and place on rack of broiler pan. Broil about 3 inches from heat 5 minutes; turn and broil 5 to 7 minutes more.

Strawberries with Kirsch

1   **pint fresh strawberries, halved**
½   **cup shredded coconut**
2   **tablespoons kirsch**

In medium bowl combine all ingredients. Stir to coat strawberries. Set aside or chill 20 to 30 minutes.

Zucchini with Basil

1   **pound zucchini**
1   **tablespoon salad oil**
½   **teaspoon salt**
1½   **teaspoons fresh basil or ¼ teaspoon dried**

Wash zucchini; cut each into quarters lengthwise and then into 2-inch pieces. Brush with oil; place on broiler pan with burgers. Sprinkle with salt and basil. Broil 5 minutes; turn and broil 4 to 5 more minutes.

ZUCCHINI TIPS

- *Slice zucchini; toss in green salad instead of cucumber.*
- *Stir ½ cup shredded zucchini into 1 cup deviled ham; add 1 teaspoon Worcestershire sauce; spread on party rye rounds.*
- *Add sliced zucchini into 3-bean salad along with some chopped green onion.*
- *To 1 cup plain yogurt add 2 cups matchstick zucchini, 1 teaspoon chopped dill, salt and pepper to taste.*

Poached Fish Steaks with Tarragon

SALMON, HALIBUT OR COD WITH HERBS

Simmered in a wine-and-herb broth, this flavorful fish main course is complemented by the simple goodness of wholesome vegetables.

Menu for 4

- **Poached Fish Steaks with Tarragon Stewed Tomatoes**
- **Stir-Fried Asparagus**
- **Pineapple-Blueberry Parfaits**

SHOPPING LIST

- ☐ 4 salmon, halibut or cod steaks, about 1 inch thick
- ☐ 1 pound fresh asparagus or 1 10-ounce package frozen asparagus spears
- ☐ 1 small onion
- ☐ 1 pint fresh blueberries or 1 10-ounce package frozen blueberries
- ☐ 1 bunch parsley
- ☐ 1 small piece fresh ginger (optional)
- ☐ 1 8¼-ounce can crushed pineapple in juice
- ☐ 2 16-ounce cans stewed tomatoes
- ☐ 1 8-ounce container plain low-fat yogurt
- ☐ 1 small box granola

Have on Hand
- ☐ Garlic
- ☐ Salad oil
- ☐ Tarragon
- ☐ Peppercorns
- ☐ Dry white wine

SCHEDULE

1. Prepare Poached Fish Steaks with Tarragon.
2. Heat stewed tomatoes.
3. Stir-fry asparagus.
4. Prepare Pineapple-Blueberry Parfaits.

Poached Fish Steaks with Tarragon

2 cups dry white wine
1 cup water
1 small onion, quartered
2 sprigs parsley
½ teaspoon tarragon
¼ teaspoon peppercorns
4 salmon, halibut or cod steaks, about 1 inch thick

In large skillet combine wine, water, onion, parsley, tarragon and peppercorns. Bring to a boil. Add fish in single layer. Reduce heat and simmer uncovered 15 minutes or until fish is opaque in center.

Stir-Fried Asparagus

1 pound fresh asparagus, trimmed, or 1 package (10 oz.) frozen asparagus spears
2 tablespoons salad oil
1 garlic clove, crushed
¼ teaspoon grated fresh ginger (optional)

Cut asparagus diagonally into 2-inch lengths, keeping stem ends separate. (For frozen asparagus, see note, below.) Heat oil in wok or Dutch oven. Add garlic, ginger if desired and asparagus stems. Stir-fry 1 minute. Add remaining asparagus; stir-fry 2 minutes.

Note: Cut frozen asparagus spears as directed above. Heat oil, add garlic, ginger and frozen asparagus. Stir-fry 1 minute.

Pineapple-Blueberry Parfaits

1 can (8¼ oz.) crushed pineapple in juice
1 pint fresh blueberries or 1 package (10 oz.) frozen blueberries, thawed
1 container (8 oz.) plain low-fat yogurt
½ cup granola

In blender or food processor puree the pineapple with its juice. In each of 4 parfait glasses place layers of pureed pineapple, whole blueberries, yogurt and granola. Top with a dollop of yogurt and a sprinkling of granola.

FIX-UPS FOR STEWED TOMATOES

Heat stewed tomatoes and add:
• *1 grated onion sauteed in 1 teaspoon margarine until translucent*
• *fresh basil leaves or a pinch of dried basil*
• *crushed tarragon leaves or crumbled oregano*
• *a sprinkling of shredded green onion*
• *flavored croutons*
• *fresh mint*
• *Pinch of grated lemon peel*

Stir-Fry with Broccoli and Red Peppers

A FLAVORFUL SKILLET DINNER

A little thinly-sliced pork loin goes a long way, in combination with the added protein of tofu (soybean curd) and almonds, which also add crunch to this colorful stir-fry dish.

Menu for 4

- **Stir-Fry with Broccoli and Red Peppers Rice**

- **Sprout-Radish Salad Lime Ice and Fortune Cookies**

SHOPPING LIST

- ☐ ¼ pound lean pork loin
- ☐ 1 pound tofu
- ☐ 1 bunch green onions
- ☐ 1 bunch broccoli
- ☐ 2 red peppers
- ☐ 1 head romaine lettuce
- ☐ 1 bunch watercress
- ☐ 1 bunch radishes
- ☐ 1 pint bean sprouts
- ☐ 1 small piece fresh ginger
- ☐ 1 small can or package whole almonds
- ☐ 1 small jar sesame seed
- ☐ 1 small bottle sesame oil
- ☐ 1 pint lime ice
- ☐ 1 small package fortune cookies

Have on Hand
- ☐ Sugar

- ☐ Cornstarch
- ☐ Long-grain rice
- ☐ Garlic
- ☐ Cider vinegar
- ☐ Distilled white vinegar
- ☐ Soy sauce
- ☐ Red pepper sauce

SCHEDULE

1. Prepare sauce and marinate tofu.
2. Cook rice.
3. Prepare Sprout-Radish Salad and dressing.
4. Stir-fry tofu, pork, peppers and broccoli.

Stir-Fry with Broccoli and Red Peppers

¼   cup soy sauce
¼   cup water
2   teaspoons sugar
1   tablespoon cider vinegar
¼   teaspoon red pepper sauce
1   teaspoon grated fresh
      ginger
1   garlic clove, crushed
1   pound tofu
¼   pound lean pork loin,
      thinly sliced
3   tablespoons salad oil
½   cup chopped green onions
1   garlic clove, crushed
1   head broccoli, cut into
      florets (save stalks for
      another use)
2   red peppers, cut into ¾-
      inch pieces
⅓   cup toasted almonds
1   tablespoons cornstarch dis-
      solved in ½ cup water

In small bowl combine first seven ingredients for sauce. With paper towels, blot excess water from tofu; cut into ½-inch cubes. Combine in small bowl with ¼ cup sauce and sliced pork. Marinate 15 to 20 minutes.

In wok or heavy skillet heat oil over high heat. Add green onions and garlic; stir-fry 1 minute. Add broccoli and red peppers; stir-fry 1 minute more until broccoli turns bright green. Add reserved sauce; cover and cook 2 to 3 minutes. Gently stir in tofu, almonds and corn-starch mixture; heat to boiling. Cook until thickened, stirring occasionally, about 2 minutes.

Sprout-Radish Salad

3   cups romaine lettuce
1   cup watercress leaves
⅔   cup thinly sliced radishes
⅔   cup fresh bean sprouts
1½   tablespoons finely
        chopped green onions
¾   teaspoon sugar
1½   tablespoons distilled
        white vinegar
2¼   teaspoons soy sauce
2¼   teaspoons water
1½   teaspoons sesame oil
⅛   teaspoon grated fresh
        ginger

In serving bowl combine all vegetables. In small jar with tight-fitting lid combine remaining ingredients; cover and shake well. Pour over salad and toss.

BEAN SPROUT SALADS

- *Toss bean sprouts with chunks of Swiss cheese, tomato and avocado.*
- *Arrange beet slices, shredded carrots and bean sprouts on lettuce leaves.*
- *Mix bean sprouts with green onion strips and pimiento strips; toss with salt, pepper and a dash each of soy sauce and sesame oil.*

Broiled Whitefish Fillets

FISH WITH FRESH HERBS, VEGETABLES AND FRUIT

Use any fresh white-fleshed fish fillets to make this light but satisfying entree. The green beans get their faint licorice flavor from chervil.

Menu for 4

- **Broiled Whitefish Fillets**
- **Small Baked Potatoes with Yogurt**

- **Green Beans with Chervil**
- **Fresh Strawberries and Sliced Bananas**

SHOPPING LIST

- ☐ 4   whitefish fillets (about 1½ pounds)
- ☐ 1   pound fresh green beans or 1 20-ounce bag frozen whole green beans
- ☐ 12   small new potatoes (about 1½ pounds)
- ☐ 2   lemons
- ☐ 1   pint strawberries
- ☐ 2   bananas
- ☐ 1   bunch fresh dill or dillweed
- ☐ 1   8-ounce container plain yogurt

Have on Hand
- ☐   Salt

- ☐   Pepper
- ☐   Garlic
- ☐   Margarine
- ☐   Dried chervil
- ☐   Paprika

SCHEDULE

1. Bake potatoes.
2. Prepare Green Beans with Chervil.
3. Prepare Broiled Whitefish Fillets with Lemon and Dill.
4. Slice strawberries and bananas.

Broiled Whitefish Fillets with Lemon and Dill

4   whitefish fillets (about
      1½ lbs.)
½   cup water
      Juice of 1 lemon
2   tablespoons chopped fresh
      dill or 2 teaspoons
      dillweed
½   garlic clove, crushed
      Lemon wedges for garnish
      Dill sprigs for garnish

Preheat broiler. Place fish in baking or broiling pan. In measuring cup combine water, lemon juice, dill and garlic; pour over fish. Broil 5 to 8 minutes, or until fish flakes when tested with fork. Place fish fillets on serving platter. Garnish with lemon wedges and dill sprigs.

Green Beans with Chervil

1   pound fresh green beans,
      trimmed, or 1 bag (20
      oz.) frozen whole green
      beans
½   teaspoon chervil
2   teaspoons margarine

Cook green beans in boiling salted water 8 to 10 minutes, until just tender-crisp. (If using frozen beans, cook according to package directions.) Drain and toss with chervil. Top with margarine.

Small Baked Potatoes with Yogurt

12   small new potatoes,
        washed
¼   cup plain yogurt
        Dash paprika

Preheat oven to 350° F. Bake potatoes for 25 to 30 minutes. Split potatoes, top with yogurt and sprinkle with paprika.

DILL TIPS

Fresh dill is now available in most supermarkets year round. Dried dillweed is an acceptable substitute, but don't confuse it with the hard round dill seeds used for pickling cucumbers. Long used as a flavor enhancer, dill makes a good salt substitute for low-sodium diets. Dill freezes well; chop before thawing and use like fresh dill. Add dill to tomato juice, fish and yellow or white vegetables.

Healthy Turkey Heroes

A NUTRITIOUS SOUP-AND-SANDWICH SUPPER

This soup is made of fresh peas, lettuce and mint; it gets its creamy texture from wholesome low-fat buttermilk. Serve it with hero rolls packed with turkey, avocado and fresh vegetables. Round out the meal with ripe, juicy pears.

===== **Menu for 4** =====

- **Spring Green Pea Soup**
- **Healthy Turkey Heroes**

- **Poppy-Seed Slaw**
  Fresh Pears

SHOPPING LIST

- ¾ pound sliced cooked turkey
- 2 small onions
- 1 pound carrots
- 1 small head cabbage
- 1 head Boston lettuce
- 2 large tomatoes
- 2½ pounds fresh green peas or 1 10-ounce package frozen tiny peas
- 1 bunch fresh mint
- 1 large avocado
- 1 small package alfalfa sprouts
- 4 ripe pears
- 4 6-inch crusty hero rolls
- 1 13¾- or 14½-ounce can chicken broth
- 1 quart buttermilk

Have on Hand
- Margarine
- Nutmeg
- Salad oil
- White vinegar
- Salt
- Pepper
- Sugar

SCHEDULE

1. Prepare Spring Green Pea Soup.
2. Prepare Healthy Turkey Heroes.
3. Prepare Poppy-Seed Slaw.

Spring Green Pea Soup

2   tablespoons chopped onion
½   cup shredded Boston lettuce
2½   pounds fresh green peas,
        shelled, or 1 package
        (10 oz.) frozen tiny peas
3   sprigs fresh mint (about
        18 leaves)
     Dash nutmeg
1   can (13¾ or 14½ oz.)
        chicken broth
½   cup buttermilk

In medium saucepan combine onion, lettuce, peas, mint, nutmeg and chicken broth; heat to boiling. Reduce heat to low; cover and simmer 15 minutes or until vegetables are very tender. Place soup in food processor or blender; process or blend until pureed and smooth. Strain. Stir in buttermilk, return to saucepan and heat through.

Healthy Turkey Heroes

4   crusty hero rolls (6 in.)
2   tablespoons margarine,
        divided
4   large lettuce leaves
2   large tomatoes, thinly sliced
1   large avocado, peeled and
        sliced
¾   pound sliced cooked turkey
1   cup alfalfa sprouts

Cut rolls in half lengthwise and spread each with 1½ tablespoons margarine.

Layer bottom half of each roll with 1 lettuce leaf, 2 tomato slices, 2 avocado slices, turkey slices, 2 more tomato slices and ¼ cup alfalfa sprouts. Cover with top half of roll.

Poppy-Seed Slaw

3   cups (about ¾ pound)
        grated cabbage
1   cup grated carrots
¼   cup chopped onion
½   teaspoon poppy seed
2   tablespoons salad oil
2   tablespoons white vinegar
2   teaspoons sugar
1   teaspoon salt
⅛   teaspoon pepper

In a medium bowl combine cabbage, carrots, onion and poppy seed; toss lightly. In small jar with tight-fitting lid combine oil, vinegar, sugar, salt and pepper; shake until well combined. Pour over cabbage. Toss again.

ADD CRUNCH WITH ALFALFA SPROUTS

- *Try sprouts in place of lettuce the next time you make bacon, lettuce and tomato sandwiches.*
- *Mix sprouts with shredded carrots for a quick and nourishing salad.*
- *Toss a handful of sprouts and some grated Cheddar cheese into a batch of scrambled eggs; serve in toasted pita rounds.*

Baked Salmon Steaks

FISH WITH VITAMIN-RICH VEGETABLES AND FRUIT

Top fresh or frozen salmon with grated onion and a bit of Worcestershire sauce and pop into the oven. Then whip up a salad of crisp greens and a saucy vegetable accompaniment.

Menu for 4

Baked Salmon Steaks with Grated Onion and Worcestershire Sauce

- **Broccoli with Mock Hollandaise Sauce**
- **Chicory and Romaine Salad**
- **Strawberry Whip**

SHOPPING LIST

- ☐ 4 salmon steaks
- ☐ 1 small onion
- ☐ 1 bunch broccoli
- ☐ 1 small head chicory
- ☐ 1 medium head romaine lettuce
- ☐ 1 pint fresh strawberries
- ☐ 1 lime
- ☐ 1 8-ounce container low-fat cottage cheese

Have on Hand
- ☐ Confectioners' sugar
- ☐ Salt
- ☐ Pepper
- ☐ Eggs

- ☐ Margarine
- ☐ Olive oil
- ☐ 1 lemon or lemon juice
- ☐ Worcestershire sauce
- ☐ Dry mustard
- ☐ Almond extract

SCHEDULE

1. Bake salmon steaks.
2. Prepare Strawberry Whip.
3. Prepare salad and dressing.
4. Cook Broccoli with Mock Hollandaise Sauce.

Broccoli with Mock Hollandaise Sauce

1   bunch broccoli, trimmed
    and cut into florets
3   tablespoons margarine
1   cup low-fat cottage cheese
2   egg yolks
¼   teaspoon dry mustard
1   tablespoon lemon juice

Cook broccoli in boiling salted water 5 to 8 minutes until tender-crisp but still bright green. Drain well. In top of double boiler melt margarine over boiling water. Add cottage cheese; heat and stir until warm. In blender beat egg yolks slightly. Gradually add warm cottage cheese and dry mustard. Blend until smooth. Transfer to bowl and stir in lemon juice. Serve sauce over broccoli.

Chicory and Romaine Salad

1   small head chicory
1   medium head romaine
    lettuce
2   tablespoons olive oil
1   tablespoon lemon juice
1   tablespoon water
¼   teaspoon salt
⅛   teaspoon pepper

Tear chicory and romaine into bite-size pieces and combine in medium salad bowl. In small jar with tight-fitting lid combine remaining ingredients and shake well to blend. Toss salad with dressing to coat.

Strawberry Whip

1   pint strawberries, divided
3   tablespoons confectioners'
    sugar
1   teaspoon lemon juice
⅛   teaspoon almond extract
1   egg white

In blender combine 1 cup berries with confectioners' sugar, lemon juice and almond extract; blend until smooth. In large mixer bowl beat egg white until stiff. Slice remaining berries and fold into egg white. Spoon both mixtures into parfait glasses in layers. Refrigerate until serving time.

PREPARING AND STORING SALAD GREENS

Discarding unusable outer leaves, wash salad greens thoroughly under cold running water to remove all grit. Dry in salad spinner, then pat with paper towels. Store in refrigerator crisper wrapped in a terry-cloth towel or tucked inside a plastic bag with paper towels on top to absorb moisture. Use within 1 or 2 days.

Nutritious & Delicious Tips

Planning Tips for Nutritious Eating Habits

Here are some good general guidelines and several specific planning tips you can use to improve the quality and type of food you and your family eat.

1. *Eat varied and balanced meals: Select a variety of foods from the Basic Four Food Groups (Beans, Grains and Nuts; Fruits and Vegetables; Milk Products; Poultry, Fish, Meat and Eggs). Not all foods contain all of the recommended nutrients, so protect yourself by eating many types of protein, carbohydrates, fats, vitamins and minerals.*

2. *Eat food as near to its natural form as possible.*

3. *Eat less fat: Select fewer high-fat meats, such as beef and pork, and use more fish and poultry. Consume more polyunsaturated fats (vegetable oils) than saturated fats. Drink skim milk.*

4. *Eat less salt: Add only half the salt called for in recipes. Cut down on foods with visible salt. Use herbs as flavorings instead.*

5. *Eat less sugar: To reduce the amount of sugar you eat, cut down on cookies, cakes and candies. Such foods are "empty calories"—that is, carbohydrates with no significant amounts of protein, fat, vitamins or minerals.*

6. *Eat more fruits, vegetables and whole grains: These foods are good sources of vitamins and minerals. They also have a high-fiber content that is beneficial in many ways, including the risk of instestinal disease.*

7. *Read the ingredient labels of all your food products: Remember the label rule, "First is most." If your brand of margarine lists hydrogenated oil first, it will increase your blood level of cholesterol more than one that is made from less saturated fats.*

Diet Tips—Little Things Mean a Lot

There's no doubt about it: calories count. If you overeat by as little as 100 calories per day (one 4-oz. glass of wine, 9 potato chips or 3 caramels), in 12 months you could be ten pounds heavier. Here are 10 easy hints on saving that magic 100.

- *Reach for plain yogurt (135) instead of fruit yogurt (255).*
- *Tuna comes two ways—in oil and in water. Dive into water; save.*
- *Thirsty? Pour 10 oz. of club soda or Perrier water with a wedge of lime instead of tonic.*
- *If you sip two cups of coffee or tea with cream and sugar, you're over by 100. Try plain.*
- *Switch to 2 glasses of skim milk instead of regular.*
- *Chocolate craving? Forego cake (315) or ice cream (154) and nibble on 1 tablespoon chocolate chips (48).*
- *Try cinnamon-raisin toast (60-76) for breakfast rather than a donut (175).*
- *Measure how much sour cream (30 per Tbs.) you ladle on a baked potato. Better turn to plain yogurt (9 per Tbs.).*
- *Squeeze fresh lemon over cooked vegetables—nix on butter or margaine (1 Tbs., 100).*
- *Cancel mayo from your B-L-T—100 calories less.*

Better Broiling

Put a piece or two of dry bread under the rack in the broiling pan to soak up the dripped fat when you're cooking meats or bacon. This helps eliminate smoking fat—and reduces the chance of it catching fire, too.

Nutrition Tips That Pay Off at the Checkout Counter

To cut down on cost and calories, substitute ground turkey in place of hamburger for spaghetti sauce or chili. Use thinly sliced chicken breast instead of veal—but take care not to overcook; it dries out quickly.

Dilled Fillets of Sole Amandine, page 36

Dilled Fillets of Sole Amandine

OVEN-POACHED FISH ROLLS

Rely on fillets of white-fleshed fish for low-calorie nutrition and satisfying taste. These rolled fillets get their crunch from sliced almonds, and the green vegetable gets its dash of color from bright pimiento.

Menu for 4

- **Dilled Fillets of Sole Amandine Steamed New Potatoes**
- **Green Beans with Pimiento**
- **Fruit-Topped Pound Cake**

SHOPPING LIST

- ☐ 4 sole fillets (about 1½ pounds)
- ☐ Small new potatoes
- ☐ 1 bunch green onions
- ☐ 1 bunch fresh dill or dillweed
- ☐ 1 large or 2 medium peaches or nectarines
- ☐ ½ pint strawberries
- ☐ ½ pint blueberries
- ☐ 1 8-ounce container plain low-fat yogurt
- ☐ 1 9-ounce package frozen whole green beans
- ☐ 1 small can or package sliced almonds
- ☐ 1 small jar chopped pimiento

Have on Hand

- ☐ Sugar
- ☐ Salt
- ☐ Pepper
- ☐ Margarine
- ☐ Vanilla extract
- ☐ Vermouth

SCHEDULE

1. Cook Dilled Fillet of Sole Amandine.
2. Steam new potatoes.
3. Prepare Green Beans with Pimiento.
4. Prepare Fruit-Topped Pound Cake.

Dilled Fillet of Sole Amandine

3   tablespoons margarine,
      divided
1   tablespoon dry vermouth
4   sole fillets (about 1½ lbs.)
½   teaspoon salt
⅛   teaspoon pepper
1   teaspoon fresh dill or ¼
      teaspoon dillweed
¼   cup sliced almonds

Preheat oven to 425° F. Place 2 tablespoons margarine in shallow casserole in oven to melt. Remove from oven; stir in vermouth.

Cut fillets in half lengthwise. Sprinkle with salt, pepper and dill. Roll up jellyroll fashion. Dip one side in melted margarine. Stand, dipped side up, in casserole. Cover and bake 20 minutes. In small skillet saute almonds in remaining tablespoon margarine just until golden. Sprinkle over fish before serving.

Green Beans with Pimiento

1   package (9 oz.) frozen
      whole green beans
2   tablespoons chopped
      pimiento
1   tablespoon sliced green
      onion
1½ teaspoons margarine
      Dash pepper

Cook beans according to package directions. Drain; add remaining ingredients. Toss until margarine is melted.

Fruit-Topped Pound Cake

1   cup sliced peaches or
      nectarines
1   cup halved strawberries
½   cup blueberries
1   cup plain low-fat yogurt
¼   teaspoon vanilla extract
4   thin slices pound cake

In medium bowl combine fruit; set aside. In small bowl combine yogurt and vanilla extract; add to fruit and stir until fruit is coated. Spoon over cake slices.

PIMIENTO, FOR A DASH OF COLOR AND FLAVOR

• *A whole pimiento pod contains a mere 7 calories, so use this bright garnish lavishly.*
• *Lay long strips on top of poached or steamed fish fillets.*
• *Make a chain of pimiento and onion rings to decorate a dish of steamed green vegetables.*
• *Mix with chilled green beans and wax beans for a colorful two-bean salad.*
• *Add to potato, egg, or tuna salad.*

Chef's Salad, page 40

Lime Broiled Breast of Chicken, page 42

Spicy Turkey Cutlets, page 44

Fettucine with Papaya and Asparagus, page 46

Poached Oranges, page 48

Chef's Salad

CLASSIC MAIN DISH WITH A CHILLED SOUP

This vichyssoise, a warm-weather favorite, is made with carrots as well as potatoes for an interesting change of pace. The chef's salad is a tasty and nourishing summer supper; you can vary the ingredients to suit your whim.

Menu for 4

- **Carrot Vichyssoise**
- **Chef's Salad**

Rye Rolls with Caraway Seed

Banana Cupcakes

SHOPPING LIST

- ☐ ¼ pound cooked ham or tongue
- ☐ ¼ pound cooked turkey breast
- ☐ ¼ pound Swiss cheese
- ☐ 3 medium potatoes
- ☐ 2 medium carrots
- ☐ 1 leek or 1 red onion
- ☐ 1 head romaine lettuce
- ☐ 3 medium tomatoes
- ☐ 1 medium cucumber
- ☐ 1 bunch radishes
- ☐ 1 bunch parsley
- ☐ 2 13¾- or 14½-ounce cans chicken broth
- ☐ Rye rolls with caraway seed
- ☐ Banana cupcakes
- ☐ 1 pint half and half cream

Have on Hand

- ☐ Salt
- ☐ Pepper
- ☐ White pepper
- ☐ Bottled salad dressing

SCHEDULE

1. Prepare Carrot Vichyssoise; chill.
2. Assemble Chef's Salad.

Carrot Vichyssoise

1½ cups potatoes, diced
1   cup carrots, sliced
1   leek, sliced, or ⅓ red
      onion, sliced
2½ cups chicken broth
¾   cup half and half cream
¾   teaspoon salt
      Pinch white pepper
      Shredded carrot and par-
      sley sprigs for garnish

In large saucepan combine potatoes, carrots, leek or onion and chicken broth; bring to a boil and cook over medium heat 15 minutes. Pour half the mixture into blender. Cover and blend until smooth; transfer to bowl. Repeat with remainder. Add half and half cream, salt and pepper; taste for seasoning. Cover and place in freezer to chill. Serve in chilled bowls; garnish with carrot and parsley.

Chef's Salad

1   head romaine lettuce
3   medium tomatoes, cut into
      wedges
1   medium cucumber, sliced
4   radishes, trimmed and
      sliced
¼   pound sliced ham or
      tongue, cut into strips
¼   pound cooked turkey
      breast, cut into strips
¼   pound Swiss cheese, cut
      into strips
      Bottled salad dressing

Line salad platter or individual plates with romaine leaves. Arrange vegetables, meat and cheese on lettuce. Sprinkle with salad dressing.

CHEF'S SALAD VARIATIONS

- Italian-Style Chef's Salad: *Substitute Genoa salami for the turkey, prosciutto for the ham, provolone for the Swiss cheese and ripe olives for the radishes. Add roasted red peppers and sprinkle with bottled Italian dressing. Serve with Italian bread.*
- Cold Cut Chef's Salad: *Use spiced ham, chicken salami and olive loaf in place of ham and turkey.*
- Seafood Chef's Salad: *Arrange on lettuce leaves ¼ pound each crabmeat, flaked lobster meat and cold cooked shrimp; garnish with tomato wedges, cucumber slices and lemon wedges; omit cheese.*
- Chef's Salad Garnishes: *Rolled or flat anchovy fillets, hard-cooked egg wedges or slices, avocado chunks, sliced raw mushrooms, red onion rings, lemon wedges, marinated artichoke hearts, green or red pepper rings.*

Lime Broiled Breast of Chicken

CHICKEN CUTLETS WITH CORIANDER AND LIME

This easy-to-prepare entree is a refreshing change from the usual chicken dishes. While you are pre-heating the oven, toast the coriander seeds to crisp them, release more of their taste and make them easier to crush. Serve the fresh fruit dessert in a crystal bowl, for a festive touch.

Menu for 4

- **Lime Broiled Breast of Chicken**
- **Orange Rice**
- **Broccoli Florets with Toasted Almonds**

Fresh Fruit with Mint

SHOPPING LIST

- ☐ 4 chicken cutlets
- ☐ 1 bunch fresh broccoli
- ☐ 1 bunch green onions
- ☐ 2 limes
- ☐ 1 orange
- ☐ 1 bunch fresh mint
- ☐ Assorted fresh fruits such as seedless grapes, plums, bananas and apples
- ☐ 1 small can or package slivered almonds
- ☐ 1 small jar coriander seed

Have on Hand
- ☐ Salt, preferably Kosher
- ☐ Pepper

- ☐ Olive oil
- ☐ Dijon mustard
- ☐ Honey
- ☐ Fresh or frozen orange juice
- ☐ Long-grain rice

SCHEDULE

1. Start cooking Orange Rice.
2. Prepare Lime Broiled Breast of Chicken.
3. Cook Broccoli Florets with Toasted Almonds.
4. Prepare Fresh Fruit with Mint.

Lime Broiled Breast of Chicken

    4   chicken cutlets
    ½   teaspoon salt, preferably
          kosher
    ⅛   teaspoon pepper
    2   tablespoons olive oil
    1   tablespoon Dijon mustard
    1   tablespoon honey
    ⅛   teaspoon toasted coriander
          seed, crushed
    8   thin slices fresh lime, peeled

Preheat broiler. Season chicken cutlets with salt and pepper; rub lightly with oil. Broil 3 minutes on each side, or until lightly browned.

Reduce oven to 375° F. Arrange chicken in buttered baking dish. In small bowl mix mustard, honey and coriander seed. Spread mixture over chicken and top with thin slices of fresh lime. Bake 8 minutes.

Orange Rice

    1½ cups long-grain rice
    1   teaspoon salt
    2   cups water
    1   cup orange juice
    2   tablespoons coarsely
          grated orange peel

In large saucepan combine rice, salt, water and orange juice. Bring to a boil, stirring once. Reduce heat, cover and simmer until rice is tender and water has been absorbed, about 15 minutes. Stir in grated orange peel.

Broccoli Florets with Toasted Almonds

    ¼   cup slivered or sliced
          almonds
    1   bunch (about 1½ lbs.)
          broccoli

Preheat oven to 400° F. Discard broccoli leaves. If stalks are thick, peel off tough outer skin and cut off ends. Remove broccoli florets and reserve. Cut stalks into ¼-inch slices. In large saucepan or skillet bring 1 inch water to a boil. Place broccoli florets and slices in steamer basket and set in boiling water. Cover and steam about 5 minutes until tender-crisp but still bright green.

Spread almonds on cookie sheet and toast until golden, 3 to 5 minutes. Transfer broccoli from steamer basket to serving dish; top with toasted almonds.

BUYING AND STORING BROCCOLI

- *Choose broccoli spears with bright green florets; those with yellowish florets are older and likely to have a stronger taste.*
- *Pick the slenderest spears you can find; very thick spears may be tough.*
- *Serve within 3 days after purchase; store in vegetable crisper.*

Spicy Turkey Cutlets

TURKEY WITH FRAGRANT SPICES

Cinnamon, allspice and cumin lend a Middle East-ern taste and aroma to this raisin-studded turkey en-tree. Serve it with couscous or rice.

Menu for 4

- **Spicy Turkey Cutlets Couscous or Rice**
- **Minted Green Peas**
- **Cinnamon Walnut Sundaes**

SHOPPING LIST

- ☐ 1½   pounds turkey cutlets
- ☐ 1   bunch green onions
- ☐ 1   red pepper
- ☐ 1   bunch fresh mint or dried mint
- ☐ 1   13¾- or 14½-ounce can chicken broth
- ☐ 1   package or box couscous or long-grain rice
- ☐ 1   small package dark seedless raisins
- ☐ 1   small can or package chopped walnuts
- ☐ 1   10-ounce package frozen peas
- ☐ 1   pint vanilla ice milk or frozen yogurt

Have on Hand

- ☐   Confectioners' sugar
- ☐   Salt
- ☐   Dark brown sugar
- ☐   Honey
- ☐   Margarine
- ☐   Salad oil
- ☐   Cinnamon
- ☐   Whole cloves
- ☐   Allspice
- ☐   Cumin

SCHEDULE

1. Cook couscous or rice.
2. Prepare sauce for Cinnamon Walnut Sundaes.
3. Prepare Spicy Turkey Cutlets.
4. Cook Minted Green Peas.

Spicy Turkey Cutlets

2   *tablespoons salad oil*
½   *cup sliced green onions*
      with tops
1   *red pepper, cut into strips*
1½ *cups chicken broth*
1   *tablespoon dark brown sugar*
1   *teaspoon cinnamon*
1   *teaspoon allspice*
1   *teaspoon cumin*
½   *teaspoon salt*
1½ *pounds turkey cutlets*
¼   *cup dark seedless raisins*

Heat oil in 12-inch skillet. Add onions and red pepper; saute 2 to 3 minutes. Add remaining ingredients except turkey and raisins; bring to a boil. Boil gently 5 minutes. Add turkey and raisins. Cook 10 minutes longer.

Minted Green Peas

½   *cup water*
1   *tablespoon fresh mint or ½*
      teaspoon dried mint,
      divided
¼   *teaspoon salt*
1   *package (10 oz.) frozen peas*
1   *tablespoon margarine*
1   *teaspoon confectioners' sugar*

In medium saucepan combine water, mint and salt. Bring to a boil over high heat. Add peas; return to a boil. Cover; reduce heat and cook according to package directions. Drain. Toss with margarine and sugar.

Cinnamon Walnut Sundaes

½   *cup coarsely chopped*
      walnuts
3   *tablespoons honey*
1   *teaspoon cinnamon*
2   *whole cloves*
1   *pint vanilla ice milk or*
      frozen yogurt

Preheat oven to 350° F. Spread walnuts in shallow baking pan and toast in oven 6 to 8 minutes. Let cool to room temperature. In small pan combine honey, cinnamon and cloves. Heat 5 minutes; remove cloves and add walnuts. Cool mixture to room temperature. At serving time place 1 scoop ice milk or frozen yogurt in each of 4 serving dishes; top with cinnamon walnut sauce.

CUMIN TIPS

- *One of the standard ingredients in curry powder and chili powder, this powdered Middle Eastern seed adds a warm and spicy flavor to many foods.*
- *Sprinkle ground cumin over omelets or scrambled eggs.*
- *Dust shrimp or whitefish fillets with cumin before cooking.*
- *Add to cooking liquid for lamb, turkey or chicken.*

Fettuccine, Papaya and Asparagus

REFRESHING AND UNUSUAL SPRINGTIME PASTA

This innovative combination of fettuccine, a green vegetable and a tropical fruit is certain to become a favorite for entertaining as well as for family dining pleasure. The rich-tasting dessert is surprisingly low in fat and calories. Try it another time with sliced peaches, plums or other seasonal fruits.

Menu for 4

- **Fettuccine with Papaya and Asparagus**
- **Cherry Tomatoes and Sugar Snap Peas**
- **Berries with Cannoli Cream**

SHOPPING LIST

- ☐ 8 ounces fettuccine noodles
- ☐ 1 pound fresh asparagus
- ☐ 1 pint cherry tomatoes
- ☐ ½ pound sugar snap peas
- ☐ 2 or 3 lemons or lemon juice
- ☐ 1 orange
- ☐ 1 ripe papaya
- ☐ 1 pint strawberries or blueberries
- ☐ 1 medium piece fresh ginger root
- ☐ 1 15-ounce container part-skim ricotta cheese
- ☐ 1 small can or package smoke-flavored almonds

Have on Hand
- ☐ Salt
- ☐ White pepper
- ☐ Olive oil
- ☐ Sugar
- ☐ Confectioners' sugar
- ☐ Vanilla extract

SCHEDULE

1. Prepare Berries with Cannoli Cream.
2. Prepare Cherry Tomatoes and Sugar Snap Peas.
3. Prepare Fettuccine with Papaya and Asparagus.

Fettuccine with Papaya and Asparagus

8 ounces fettuccine noodles
1 pound fresh asparagus
¼ cup fresh lemon juice
2 teaspoons grated fresh ginger
¾ teaspoon sugar
½ teaspoon salt
⅛ teaspoon white pepper
2 tablespoons olive oil
1 ripe papaya, seeded, peeled and thinly sliced
¼ cup chopped smoke-flavored almonds

Cook noodles according to package directions. Drain; rinse well under cold water to cool; drain again thoroughly.

Snap off and discard tough ends of asparagus; remove scales. Rinse stalks under cold water. Cut diagonally into 1½-inch pieces; keep tips separate. In large saucepan cook asparagus stalks 3 minutes in boiling salted water. Add tips; cook 1 minute more. Drain and run under cold water to cool.

In small bowl combine lemon juice, ginger, sugar, salt and pepper. Mix well. Transfer fettuccine to large bowl. Sprinkle on lemon juice mixture. Toss well. Drizzle with olive oil; toss again. Add asparagus, papaya and half the almonds. Toss gently and transfer to serving platter. Sprinkle with remaining almonds.

Berries with Cannoli Cream

1 pint fresh strawberries or blueberries, sliced
2 teaspoons sugar
1 container (15 oz.) part-skim ricotta cheese
⅓ cup confectioners' sugar, sifted
1 teaspoon vanilla extract
1½ teaspoons grated orange peel

In small bowl toss berries with sugar; set aside. In medium bowl with mixer at high speed, whip ricotta cheese until fluffy. Beat in confectioners' sugar and vanilla; whip about 2 minutes more until smooth and light. Stir in orange peel. Divide berries among 4 dessert dishes. Top each serving with cheese mixture.

ASPARAGUS TIPS

Steamed, baked, stir-fried or boiled, this favorite springtime vegetable is not only tasty but rich in vitamins A and C. Asparagus also has some B vitamins and iron, so serve it often.

Swordfish Diablo

BROILED FISH WITH HORSERADISH AND TOMATO

This menu features nourishing foods cooked quickly to preserve vitamins and other nutrients. Steam the potatoes as well as the broccoli, if you wish, for extra food value. When swordfish is unavailable, substitute halibut or cod steaks.

Menu for 4

- **Swordfish Diablo New Potatoes with Chopped Parsley**
- **Fresh Spinach with Green Onions**
- **Poached Oranges**

SHOPPING LIST

- ☐ 1½ pounds swordfish steaks
- ☐ 2 large seedless oranges
- ☐ 1 pound fresh spinach
- ☐ 1½ pounds new potatoes
- ☐ 1 bunch parsley
- ☐ 1 bunch green onions
- ☐ 1 small can or jar slivered or sliced almonds
- ☐ 1 8-ounce container plain low-fat yogurt
- ☐ 1 6-ounce can tomato juice
- ☐ 1 small can or package flaked coconut (optional)

Have on Hand
- ☐ Sugar

- ☐ Salt
- ☐ Pepper
- ☐ Horseradish
- ☐ Worcestershire sauce
- ☐ Dry mustard
- ☐ Paprika
- ☐ Orange-flavored liqueur

SCHEDULE

1. Prepare Poached Oranges.
2. Cook potatoes.
3. Prepare Swordfish Diablo.
4. Prepare Spinach with Green Onions

Swordfish Diablo

1½ *pounds swordfish steaks*
½ *teaspoon salt*
  Dash pepper
1 *cup plain low-fat yogurt*
2 *teaspoons dry mustard*
1 *teaspoon prepared*
  horseradish
2 *tablespoons tomato juice*
  Dash Worcestershire sauce
  Dash paprika

Preheat broiler or prepare outdoor grill. Season fish with salt and pepper. Broil or grill fish steaks, turning once, 20 to 25 minutes or until it flakes easily when tested with a fork. In small bowl combine yogurt, dry mustard, horseradish, tomato juice and Worcestershire sauce. Serve over fish.

Fresh Spinach with Green Onions

1 *pound fresh spinach*
¼ *cup water*
¼ *teaspoon salt*
4 *green onions, sliced*

Tear spinach into bite-size pieces and wash thoroughly to remove all grit. In large saucepan combine spinach, water and salt. Cook over low heat 8 to 10 minutes until spinach is limp. Drain very well, squeezing out excess moisture with back of wooden spoon. Transfer to serving bowl and toss with green onions.

Poached Oranges

4 *large seedless oranges*
3½ *tablespoons sugar*
3½ *tablespoons water*
1 *tablespoon orange-*
  flavored liqueur
  Grated orange peel or
  flaked coconut for gar-
  nish (optional)

With sharp knife peel oranges, making sure to remove all layers of skin. Place oranges in medium saucepan with sugar and water. Cover, bring to a boil and simmer gently for 5 minutes. Transfer oranges to serving dish. Cook syrup down to approximately ¼ cup and pour over oranges. Refrigerate or allow to cool at room temperature. At serving time sprinkle the oranges with liqueur and garnish with grated peel or flaked coconut if desired.

POTATO TIPS

"New" potatoes are not a special variety or type; they're simply small, young potatoes with thin skin, brought to market immediately after being harvested. With potatoes of all types, the richest concentration of vitamins and minerals lies just under the skin; be careful not to remove too much of this layer when you peel— or better yet, don't peel at all.

Fruit Medley, page 52

Bombay Curry, page 54

Chicken Stir Fry, page 56

Tossed Green Salad, page 58

Turkey Piccata

ZESTY QUICK-COOKING CUTLETS

Much easier on the budget than Classic Veal Piccata, this quick and easy turkey entree is a good family or company offering.

Menu for 4

- **Turkey Piccata**
  Carrots with
      Chopped
      Parsley
- **Green Salad**
      with Low-
      Calorie
      Dressing
- **Fruit Medley**

SHOPPING LIST

- ☐ 4 turkey cutlets (about 1 pound)
- ☐ 1 pound carrots
- ☐ 1 head romaine lettuce
- ☐ 1 small head chicory
- ☐ 1 green pepper
- ☐ 1 bunch green onions
- ☐ 1 small onion
- ☐ 1 bunch fresh parsley
- ☐ 1 banana
- ☐ 1 apple
- ☐ 1 pear
- ☐ 1 orange
- ☐ 1 small bunch red or green seedless grapes
- ☐ 3 lemons
- ☐ 1 small jar India relish
- ☐ 1 6-ounce can cocktail vegetable juice
- ☐ 1 small jar apricot preserves

Have on Hand

- ☐ Salt
- ☐ Pepper
- ☐ Margarine
- ☐ Garlic
- ☐ Salad oil
- ☐ Cider vinegar
- ☐ Marjoram
- ☐ Orange-flavored liqueur

SCHEDULE

1. Prepare Green Salad and Low-calorie Dressing.
2. Prepare Fruit Medley.
3. Cook carrots.
4. Prepare Turkey Piccata.

Turkey Piccata

4	turkey cutlets (about 1 lb.), pounded
1	teaspoon marjoram, finely crumbled
½	teaspoon salt
2	tablespoons margarine, divided
1½	teaspoons salad oil
	Peel and juice of 1 lemon
1	garlic clove, finely minced
2	teaspoons chopped parsley
	Lemon slices for garnish

Lightly sprinkle both sides of cutlets with marjoram and salt. In medium skillet heat 1 tablespoon margarine and oil over medium-high heat. Sprinkle both sides of cutlets with lemon peel, garlic and parsley. Saute in hot skillet 2 to 3 minutes on each side until lightly browned. Transfer to plate; keep warm. In small saucepan heat remaining tablespoon margarine over medium-high heat until hot and foamy. Sprinkle cutlets with lemon juice and melted margarine. Garnish with lemon slices.

Green Salad with Low-Calorie Dressing

4	cups romaine lettuce, torn into bite-size pieces
1	cup chicory, torn into bite-size pieces
1	green pepper, sliced

2	green onions, sliced
1	can (6 oz.) cocktail vegetable juice
2	tablespoons India relish
2	tablespoons minced onion
1	teaspoon cider vinegar
⅛	teaspoon pepper

In large salad bowl combine romaine, chicory, green pepper and green onions. In jar with tight-fitting lid combine remaining ingredients and shake to blend. Toss salad with dressing at serving time.

Fruit Medley

2	tablespoons lemon juice.
2	tablespoons orange-flavored liqueur
1	tablespoon apricot preserves
1	medium banana, sliced
½	apple, sliced
½	pear, sliced
½	cup orange sections
½	cup seedless red or green grapes, halved

In large bowl combine lemon juice, orange liqueur and apricot preserves. Stir until blended. Add fruit and toss to coat. Chill until serving time.

MARJORAM TIPS

This herb, similar to oregano, is available either dried or ground, and adds delicate flavor to chicken or turkey. You can also add it to:
- *carrots, cauliflower or summer squash*
- *stuffing for turkey or chicken*

Bombay Curry

PROTEIN-PACKED INDIAN CURRY

Both chick-peas and rice contain protein. When combined in this spicy curry, the two complement each other to form a balanced-protein meal. Serve the dish with long-grain rice and Raita, the traditional cucumber-yogurt accompaniment.

Menu for 4

- **Bombay Curry with Rice**
- **Raita**
  Chutney
- **Fruit Parfaits**

SHOPPING LIST

- ☐ 1 cantaloupe
- ☐ 1 pint fresh blueberries or 1 10-ounce package frozen blueberries
- ☐ 1 medium onion
- ☐ 1 medium cucumber
- ☐ 1 pound carrots or 2 10-ounce packages frozen sliced carrots
- ☐ 1 head cauliflower or 1 10-ounce package frozen cauliflower florets
- ☐ 1 6-ounce can or small bottle apple juice
- ☐ 1 bottle chutney
- ☐ 1 20-ounce can chick-peas or garbanzo beans
- ☐ 1 8-ounce container plain low-fat yogurt
- ☐ 1 10-ounce package frozen green peas
- ☐ 1 pint vanilla frozen yogurt or ice milk

Have on Hand

- ☐ Sugar
- ☐ Salt
- ☐ Long-grain rice
- ☐ Milk
- ☐ Salad oil
- ☐ Curry powder
- ☐ Cumin

SCHEDULE

1. Prepare Bombay Curry.
2. Cook rice.
3. Prepare Raita.
4. Prepare Fruit Parfaits.

Bombay Curry with Rice

1	can (20 oz.) chick-peas or garbanzo beans, with their liquid
2	tablespoons salad oil
½	cup chopped onion
4	teaspoons curry powder
¾	cup milk
2	cups cauliflower florets
2	medium carrots, peeled and sliced
1	package (10 oz.) frozen green peas
1	teaspoon salt
2	tablespoons apple juice
3	cups cooked rice

Drain chick-peas and measure liquid. Add enough water to equal 1 cup. Set aside. In medium saucepan heat oil over medium heat. Add onion and saute until translucent, about 5 minutes. Reduce heat to low; add curry powder and cook, stirring constantly, 5 minutes. Add chick-pea liquid, milk, cauliflower and carrots. Simmer until vegetables are tender, about 10 minutes. Add chick-peas, green peas, salt and apple juice. Continue cooking 5 minutes. Serve over rice.

Raita

1	medium cucumber, peeled, seeded and chopped
¼	teaspoon salt
1	cup plain low-fat yogurt
⅛	teaspoon cumin

In small bowl combine all ingredients. Set aside until serving time.

Fruit Parfaits

½	cantaloupe, cut into chunks
1	pint vanilla frozen yogurt or ice milk
1	cup fresh or frozen blueberries

Wash blueberries or thaw if frozen. Divide half the cantaloupe chunks into 4 dessert bowls. Top with 1 scoop frozen yogurt or ice milk. Spoon on remaining cantaloupe. Sprinkle with blueberries.

RICE TIPS

This mainstay of the diet of more than half the people in the world is filling, nourishing, inexpensive, easy to prepare and surprisingly low in calories:

- *½ cup of plain rice contains only 82 calories*
- *It's also low in fat, cholesterol and sodium*
- *Provides some B-complex vitamins and iron*
- *Rice is 98 percent digestible and helps the system digest complex proteins in other foods*

Chicken Stir-Fry

TENDER CHICKEN WITH ORIENTAL VEGETABLES

The sauce for this Chinese entree is enhanced with soy and ginger for that distinctive Asian flavor. For a fresh finale, offer a colorful presentation of fruit.

═══ Menu for 4 ═══

● **Chicken Stir-Fry**
  Marinated
   Cucumbers
   and Onions

  Rice
● **Pineapple**
   Strawberry
   Boats

SHOPPING LIST

- ☐ 4 chicken cutlets
- ☐ 1 small red onion
- ☐ 1 medium cucumber
- ☐ 1 head lettuce
- ☐ 2 tomatoes
- ☐ 1 ripe pineapple
- ☐ 1 pint strawberries
- ☐ 1 bunch fresh mint
- ☐ 1 bunch fresh basil or dried basil
- ☐ 1 13¾- or 14½-ounce can chicken broth
- ☐ 1 10- or 14-ounce package frozen Oriental vegetables

Have on Hand
- ☐ Long-grain rice
- ☐ Cornstarch
- ☐ Sugar
- ☐ Salt

- ☐ Salad oil
- ☐ Distilled white vinegar
- ☐ Soy sauce
- ☐ Ginger
- ☐ Red pepper
- ☐ Honey
- ☐ Dry sherry
- ☐ Black raspberry or orange liqueur (optional)

SCHEDULE

1. Cook rice.
2. Prepare Marinated Cucumbers and Onions.
3. Prepare Pineapple Strawberry Boats.
4. Cook Chicken Stir-Fry.

Chicken Stir-Fry

  4   *chicken cutlets*
  ½ *cup chicken broth*
  2   *tablespoons dry sherry*
  2   *tablespoons soy sauce*
  1   *tablespoon sugar*
      Dash ground ginger
      Dash ground red pepper
  1   *tablespoon cornstarch*
  1   *tablespoon salad oil*
  1   *package (10 or 14 oz.)*
      frozen Oriental
      vegetables
  2   *tablespoons water*

Thinly slice the chicken cutlets; place in shallow bowl. In medium bowl combine chicken broth, sherry, soy sauce, sugar, ginger and red pepper. Stir well and pour 2 tablespoons over sliced chicken; marinate 10 minutes. Add cornstarch to remaining sauce; set aside. In large skillet heat salad oil. Add chicken; stir-fry. Add frozen vegetables and water. Cover and simmer 2 minutes. Stir sauce and add to skillet. Boil 1 minute, stirring constantly.

Pineapple Strawberry Boats

  1 *large ripe pineapple*
  1 *tablespoon honey*
  1 *pint strawberries*
  2 *tablespoons black raspberry*
     or orange liqueur
     (optional)
     Fresh mint leaves for
     garnish

Using a very sharp, heavy knife, cut pineapple and leaves lengthwise through center. With a grapefruit knife cut around edges of each half, leaving a ¼-inch shell. Remove and discard tough core. Cut out the fruit and invert shells to drain. Cut pineapple into cubes and place in large bowl; add honey. Hull and wash strawberries and cut in half if large. Place in bowl and toss with liqueur, if desired. At serving time combine berries with pineapple chunks and spoon into pineapple shells. Garnish with mint leaves.

PINEAPPLE SHELL DESSERTS

- *Toss pineapple chunks with blueberries, kiwi slices, fresh cherries, purple grapes, sliced plums or fresh raspberries. Sweeten with honey if necessary and flavor with orange liqueur, kirsch, amaretto or crème de cassis, if you wish.*
- *Fruit-filled pineapple shells also make a good party dish; spear chunks of pineapple and other fruit with picks and let guests help themselves.*

La Strata

BEEF CASSEROLE WITH MOZZARELLA CHEESE

This entree heats in the oven while you prepare the rest of the meal. Follow the hearty casserole with a nutritious frozen tofu-based dessert.

Menu for 4

- **La Strata**
- **Tossed Green Salad**
- **Whole Wheat French Bread**
- **Whole Earth Sundaes**

SHOPPING LIST

- ☐ 1 onion
- ☐ 2 heads Bibb or Boston lettuce
- ☐ 1 green pepper
- ☐ 1 small cucumber
- ☐ 1 bunch watercress
- ☐ 1 bunch fresh parsley or dried parsley
- ☐ 1 bunch fresh basil or dried basil
- ☐ 1 lemon or bottled lemon juice
- ☐ 1 8-ounce can tomato sauce
- ☐ 1 4-ounce can mushrooms
- ☐ 1 small package granola
- ☐ 1 small package sunflower seeds
- ☐ Whole wheat French bread
- ☐ 1 4-ounce package shredded skim-milk mozzarella cheese
- ☐ 1 8-ounce container low-fat cottage cheese
- ☐ 1 pint frozen tofu-based dessert, any flavor
- ☐ 1 10-ounce package frozen chopped spinach
- ☐ 1 pound ground beef

Have on Hand

- ☐ Salt
- ☐ Pepper
- ☐ Garlic
- ☐ Dijon mustard
- ☐ Oregano
- ☐ 1 lemon or lemon juice
- ☐ Olive oil
- ☐ Salad oil
- ☐ White wine vinegar

SCHEDULE

1. Prepare La Strata.
2. Prepare Tossed Green Salad and Dressing.
3. Prepare Whole Earth Sundaes.

La Strata

1   package (10 oz.) frozen
    chopped spinach
1   pound ground beef
1/4   cup minced onion
1   small garlic clove, minced
1   can (8 oz.) tomato sauce
1   tablespoon chopped fresh
    basil or 1 teaspoon dried
1   tablespoon chopped fresh
    parsley or 1 teaspoon dried
1/4   teaspoon oregano
    Dash pepper
1   can (4 oz.) mushrooms,
    drained
1   container (8 oz.) low-fat
    cottage cheese
1   package (4 oz.) shredded
    skim-milk mozzarella cheese

Preheat oven to 375° F. In saucepan cook spinach in small amount of water until thawed; drain well. In medium skillet saute ground beef, onion and garlic until onion is translucent and beef is browned. Add tomato sauce, basil, parsley, oregano, pepper and mushrooms. In medium bowl combine spinach and cottage cheese. In 8-inch square baking dish arrange in layers spinach mixture, meat mixture and mozzarella cheese. Repeat layering, ending with cheese. Bake 15 to 20 minutes or until hot and bubbly.

Tossed Green Salad

1   tablespoon olive oil

1   tablespoon salad oil
1   tablespoon white wine
    vinegar
1   tablespoon water
1/8   teaspoon salt
    Dash pepper
1/2   teaspoon fresh lemon juice
1/2   teaspoon Dijon mustard
5   cups (1 head) torn Bibb or
    Boston lettuce
1   bunch watercress, trimmed
    and coarsely chopped
1   green pepper, sliced
1   small cucumber, sliced

In small jar with tight-fitting lid combine oils, vinegar, water, salt, pepper, lemon juice and mustard; shake well to combine.

In medium bowl combine lettuce, watercress, pepper, and cucumber slices. Add dressing and toss.

Whole Earth Sundaes

1   pint frozen tofu-based
    dessert, any flavor
4   tablespoons granola
4   tablespoons toasted sun-
    flower seeds

Place 1 scoop frozen tofu-based dessert in each of 4 dessert dishes. Top each with 1 tablespoon granola and sunflower seeds.

GARLIC TIP

Whenever possible, use garlic cloves rather than garlic salt or powder for tastier dishes with better flavor.

Turkey Vegetable Platter, page 62

Turkey Vegetable Platter

TURKEY BREAST WITH VEGETABLES

This colorful entree can be a fast family dinner for a busy day or a company luncheon spread. Vary the condiment according to the occasion—yogurt for one meal, low-cal mayonnaise for another, chick-pea dip for a third. Add olives, if you like.

══ Menu for 4 ══

- **Turkey Vegetable Platter**
- **Whole Wheat Rolls**
- **Black Beauty Sundaes**

SHOPPING LIST

- ☐ ¾ pound sliced cooked turkey breast
- ☐ 8 small new potatoes
- ☐ 1 pound carrots
- ☐ ½ pound fresh green beans
- ☐ ¼ pound snow peas
- ☐ 1 pint cherry tomatoes
- ☐ ½ pint blackberries or 1 package frozen blackberries
- ☐ Whole wheat rolls
- ☐ 1 8-ounce container plain low-fat yogurt or 1 16-ounce jar imitation mayonnaise
- ☐ 1 pint vanilla ice milk, frozen yogurt or frozen tofu-based dessert

Have on Hand

- ☐ Sugar
- ☐ Blackberry brandy

SCHEDULE

1. Steam vegetables and cool separately.
2. Arrange Turkey Vegetable Platter.
3. Prepare Black Beauty Sundaes.

Turkey Vegetable Platter

8   small new potatoes,
      washed and halved
1   pound carrots halved
      crosswise then
      lengthwise
½   pound fresh green beans,
      trimmed
¼   pound snow peas, trimmed
1   pint cherry tomatoes,
      trimmed
¾   pound sliced cooked turkey
      breast
      **Plain low-fat yogurt or
      imitation mayonnaise**

Place potatoes in steamer basket over boiling salted water and steam 4 minutes. Add carrots and continue steaming about 3 minutes more. Add green beans and cook 4 to 5 minutes more. Add snow peas and steam 1 minute longer. Remove from heat and refresh vegetables separately, under cold water. Drain on paper towels.

Arrange steamed vegetables with tomatoes and sliced turkey breast on large platter with small bowl of plain low-fat yogurt or imitation mayonnaise.

Black Beauty Sundaes

2   tablespoons blackberry
      brandy
2   teaspoons sugar
½   pint fresh or frozen
      blackberries
1   pint vanilla ice milk,
      frozen yogurt or
      frozen tofu-based
      dessert

In small bowl mix blackberry brandy with sugar; add blackberries and marinate at room temperature about 30 minutes. At serving time place 1 scoop ice milk, frozen yogurt or tofu-based dessert in each of 4 dessert dishes. Top with blackberry mixture.

POTATO TIPS

Potatoes will keep for several weeks in a dry, dark, well-ventilated place at about 45° F.

- *If you have no such place to store them, you'll do best to buy small amounts of potatoes as you need them.*
- *When stored at room temperature, potatoes will begin to sprout and shrivel within 10 days or so.*
- *If you refrigerate potatoes at a temperature below 45° F. for more than a week, they are likely to develop a sweet taste, because cold air will turn some of the starch into sugar.*

More Diet Tips

Here are some more ideas for making dieting easier and making nutritious and delicious foods part of good eating every day.

- *Teach your kids (and yourself) to reach for carrot, celery, cucumber or green pepper sticks instead of potato chips, pretzels, nuts or crackers.*
- *Make delicious desserts of fresh fruit a family habit.*
- *Serve more chicken and fish, less red meat. Serve fresh fruits and vegetables, especially in season, when the price is right.*
- *Don't think of the word "diet". Think instead of eating things that are good for you. Moderation is the key. A bite of chocolate cake will not make you fat (but be careful—too many bites will).*
- *Include milk for your children with each meal. Adults should substitute low-fat or skimmed milk for whole milk.*
- *Learn the joys of plain yogurt as a lower calorie substitute for sour cream, heavy cream, mayonnaise. To thicken a soup, make a salad dressing, marinade a chicken, top a baked potato.*
- *Poach, steam or broil fish and meats instead of frying.*
- *Don't forget eye-appeal when serving. Mix colors, textures. Add a sprig of parsley, a wedge of lemon, a twist of lime to decorate a plate.*
- *Simplify cooking—even when you entertain.*

Frozen Dessert Tips

- *Ice cream, which tastes sinfully good, can be good for you, in moderation. The wholesome milk and rich cream make it high in protein, calcium and riboflavin, all essential to good health. Minimum requirement for ice cream is 10 percent milk fat. With the stirring in of egg yolks, it's called French ice cream or frozen custard.*
- *Ice milk has less fat (2-7 percent) and fewer calories.*
- *Sherbet has even less milk fat (1-2 percent).*
- *Water ices contain no trace of dairy products.*

Shake the Salt Habit

Statistics show Americans consume 10 to 30 times the amount of sodium our bodies need, so start thinking twice before passing the salt. Instead, spice up your meals with these easy ideas.

- *Hide the salt shaker—keep a pepper mill, hot pepper sauce or blend of mixed herbs handy.*
- *Make things better with bitters. Splash the aromatic liquid into burgers, stews, soups, salt-free seltzer or juices.*
- *Boost baked fish or chicken with tangy citrus—lemons, oranges, grapefruit, limes. Squeeze into marinades, salad dressings.*
- *Sprinkle a variety of vinegars (tarragon, rice wine, herb) and oils (sesame, walnut, hazelnut) on salads, vegetables.*
- *Create your own meat sauces. Brush on a paste of dry mustard, lemon juice or pepper before cooking; chopped tomato, onion, cumin or chili pepper after broiling. Or try horseradish or plain yogurt.*

How to Peel, Seed and Slice Cucumbers

With vegetable peeler peel off tough skin. Cut cucumber in half lengthwise and scoop out seeds with a melonball cutter or small metal spoon. Place cut side down and then slice into crescents.

Pineapple Serving Boats

1. *Choose a plump, slightly firm fruit. Holding pineapple securely, halve lengthwise, cutting through flesh and leaves, then quarter.*
2. *Cut the fibrous core from each quarter and discard. Then cut carefully underneath the flesh, leaving behind a half-inch-deep shell as the hull of your boat.*
3. *Cut flesh crosswise into bite-size pieces. Serve the pineapple chunks in shell, interspersed with strawberries or melon chunks, if desired.*

Fish Salad Verde

FISH FILLETS WITH FRESH ASPARAGUS

Low in sodium and fat and high in vitamins, this main-dish salad can be served warm, chilled or at room temperature. It's equally good when you make it with poached sole, snapper, halibut or salmon instead of the flounder used in this recipe.

Menu for 4

- **Fish Salad Verde**
- **Natural Asparagus**
- **Whole Wheat Crisps**
  Orange Ice

SHOPPING LIST

- ☐ 1 pound flounder fillets
- ☐ 1 pound fresh spinach
- ☐ 1 pound fresh asparagus
- ☐ 2 medium tomatoes
- ☐ 1 lime
- ☐ 1 loaf thinly sliced whole wheat bread
- ☐ 1 small jar sesame seed
- ☐ 1 8-ounce container plain low-fat yogurt
- ☐ 1 pint orange ice

Have on Hand
- ☐ Sugar

- ☐ Salt
- ☐ Pepper
- ☐ Margarine
- ☐ Salad oil
- ☐ Dijon mustard
- ☐ Tarragon

SCHEDULE

1. Prepare Natural Asparagus.
2. Prepare Fish Salad Verde.
3. Bake Whole Wheat Crisps.

Fish Salad Verde

1 **pound fresh spinach**
1 **pound flounder fillets**
1 **tablespoon Dijon mustard**
¼ **cup salad oil**
   Juice and grated peel of 1 lime
½ **teaspoon tarragon**
½ **teaspoon sugar**
   Dash salt
   Dash pepper
¼ **cup plain low-fat yogurt**
2 **medium tomatoes, cut into**
      wedges

Wash spinach thoroughly and pat dry. Finely chop enough spinach to measure ¼ cup; set aside.

In large, deep skillet bring 1 inch water to a boil. Add flounder fillets; cover and reduce heat to medium. Poach fish 5 to 10 minutes or until it flakes easily when tested with a fork. Remove from poaching liquid and set aside.

In medium bowl place mustard. Gradually beat in oil with wire whisk until blended. Add lime juice and peel, chopped spinach, tarragon, sugar, salt and pepper; beat well. Stir in yogurt. Arrange reserved whole spinach leaves on large platter. Break fish into pieces and place on spinach; surround with tomato wedges. Spoon dressing over fish and vegetables.

Natural Asparagus

1 **pound fresh asparagus**
½ **teaspoon salt**
⅛ **teaspoon pepper**

2 **tablespoons margarine**

Preheat oven to 350° F. Rinse and trim asparagus; peel only if stalks are tough. Place asparagus in 1 or 2 layers in flat baking dish. Sprinkle with salt and pepper to taste and dot with margarine. Cover tightly with foil and bake 25 minutes.

Whole Wheat Crisps

4 **thin slices whole wheat**
      bread
4 **teaspoons margarine**
2 **teaspoons toasted sesame**
      seed

Preheat oven to 350° F. Trim crusts from bread, place slices on cookie sheet and bake 5 to 7 minutes or until crisp. Spread each slice lightly with margarine and sprinkle with sesame seed.

START WITH A CONTAINER OF PLAIN YOGURT

- Georgian Borscht: *Whirl yogurt in blender with 1 small can diced beets, 1 cup bottled borscht, grated lemon peel and salt and pepper to taste.*
- Fruit Salad Dressing: *Stir together ½ cup plain yogurt, ¼ cup ricotta cheese, ¼ cup orange juice and 1 ½ tablespoons grated orange peel.*

Shrimp with Avocado

SEAFOOD SALAD WITH HOMEMADE MELBA TOAST

This salad supper is packed with nutrients, yet low in fat and calories. You may wish to make a double or triple batch of Melba Toast with Dill. Save left-overs to enjoy as low-calorie snacks.

Menu for 4

- **Shrimp with Avocado**
- **Marinated Sliced Tomatoes**
- **Melba Toast with Dill**
- **Berry Sherbet or Ice**

SHOPPING LIST

- ☐ 1 pound cooked medium shrimp
- ☐ 1 bunch celery
- ☐ 2 medium tomatoes
- ☐ 2 ripe avocados
- ☐ 1 head leafy greens
- ☐ 1 bunch fresh parsley
- ☐ 1 bunch fresh dill or dillweed
- ☐ 2 lemons
- ☐ 1 loaf seedless rye bread
- ☐ 1 pint strawberry sherbet or ice

- ☐ Margarine
- ☐ Salad oil
- ☐ Cider vinegar
- ☐ Worcestershire sauce
- ☐ Red pepper sauce
- ☐ Ketchup
- ☐ Horseradish
- ☐ Oregano

Have on Hand

- ☐ Sugar
- ☐ Salt
- ☐ Pepper
- ☐ Garlic

SCHEDULE

1. Prepare Marinated Sliced Tomatoes.
2. Prepare Melba Toast with Dill.
3. Prepare Shrimp with Avocado.

Shrimp with Avocado

1 **pound cooked medium shrimp, shelled and deveined**
½ **cup sliced celery**
1 **cup ketchup**
2 **tablespoons horseradish**
1 **teaspoon lemon juice**
¼ **teaspoon Worcestershire sauce**
¼ **teaspoon red pepper sauce**
2 **ripe avocados, peeled, pitted and cut into chunks**
Lemon juice
Leafy greens
Lemon slices for garnish
Fresh parsley for garnish

In medium bowl combine shrimp and celery. In small bowl combine ketchup, horseradish, lemon juice, Worcestershire sauce and red pepper sauce. Spoon half the dressing over shrimp. Toss; cover and refrigerate until serving time.

Arrange leafy greens on large platter and mound shrimp salad in center. Arrange avocado chunks around shrimp salad. Sprinkle with lemon juice; garnish with lemon slices and parsley. Pass reserved dressing.

Marinated Sliced Tomatoes

3 **tablespoons salad oil**
2 **tablespoons cider vinegar**
1 **tablespoon minced parsley**
1 **small garlic clove, finely minced**

½ **teaspoon sugar**
⅛ **teaspoon oregano**
Dash pepper
2 **medium tomatoes, thinly sliced**

In cup or small bowl combine all ingredients except tomatoes. Arrange tomato slices on plate. Pour dressing over and cover with plastic wrap. Refrigerate until serving time.

Melba Toast with Dill

1 **teaspoon fresh dill or**
   ½ **teaspoon dillweed**
1 **tablespoon margarine**
3 **thin slices seedless rye bread**

Preheat oven to 350° F. In small bowl combine dill and margarine. Trim crusts from bread and spread each slice thinly with dill-margarine. Cut each slice crosswise into 3 narrow rectangles. Place on cookie sheet and toast in oven until crisp, 5 to 7 minutes.

WORCESTERSHIRE SAUCE TIPS

• *This spicy concoction is especially good with shrimp and other seafoods. Brush some on fish fillets before broiling for extra taste.*
• *Make a fast chutney-type condiment by adding a few shakes to applesauce, along with a handful of golden raisins.*

Chicken Piquante

SPICY CHICKEN CUTLETS WITH RICE AND ZUCCHINI

These tender, quick-cooking chicken (or turkey, if you prefer) cutlets are simmered in a sauce of tomatoes and flavored with fragrant cloves and cinnamon. Serve them with a garlicky combination of sauteed fresh vegetables.

Menu for 4

- **Chicken Piquante**
- **Sauteed Zucchini, Green Pepper and Onion**

Rice
Lemon Sherbet with Seedless Grapes or Melon Balls

SHOPPING LIST

- □ 4 chicken cutlets
- □ 1 fresh jalapeño pepper or 1 small can jalapeño peppers
- □ 1 medium and 1 small onion
- □ 3 medium zucchini
- □ 1 large green pepper
- □ 1 small bunch seedless grapes or 1 small melon
- □ 1 14-ounce can tomatoes
- □ 1 small can or package slivered almonds
- □ 1 small box raisins
- □ 1 pint lemon sherbet

Have on Hand
- □ Salt
- □ Pepper

- □ Long-grain rice
- □ Margarine
- □ Garlic
- □ Salad oil
- □ Cinnamon
- □ Ground cloves

SCHEDULE

1. Prepare Chicken Piquante.
2. Cook rice.
3. Prepare Sauteed Zucchini, Green Pepper and Onion.
4. Prepare grapes or melon balls for dessert.

Chicken Piquante

1   *tablespoon salad oil,*
      divided
1/3 *cup chopped onion*
2   *garlic cloves, minced*
1   *can (14 oz.) tomatoes, cut*
      up, with juice
2½ *tablespoons raisins*
1   *fresh jalapeño pepper,*
      seeded and chopped or
      1 tablespoon canned
      jalapeño
¼   *teaspoon cinnamon*
¼   *teaspoon salt*
⅛   *teaspoon ground cloves*
⅛   *teaspoon pepper*
1½ *teaspoons margarine*
4   *chicken cutlets*
2   *tablespoons slivered*
      almonds, toasted

To prepare sauce, heat ½ teaspoon oil in large skillet. Add onion and garlic; saute 5 minutes. Stir in tomatoes and juice, jalapeño and seasonings. Simmer, stirring occasionally, over medium heat 15 minutes or until sauce thickens.

In another large skillet heat remaining oil and margarine over medium heat. Cook cutlets in single layer about 1 minute on each side. Transfer to skillet with sauce. Simmer 5 minutes, spooning sauce over chicken. Arrange on serving platter and sprinkle with toasted almonds.

Sauteed Zucchini, Green Pepper and Onion

1   *tablespoon salad oil*
1   *medium onion, sliced*
2   *garlic cloves, crushed*
3   *medium zucchini, sliced*
1   *large green pepper, seeded*
      and sliced
2   *tablespoons water*
½   *teaspoon salt*

In medium skillet heat oil. Add onion and garlic; saute 5 minutes. Add remaining ingredients; cover and simmer 10 to 15 minutes or until vegetables are tender.

SHERBET AND FRUIT DESSERTS

For icy good taste and a rainbow of colors serve imaginative combinations of sherbet, ice milk or frozen tofu-based dessert and fresh, perfect fruit. Here are some suggestions:

- *lime sherbet topped with whole strawberries*
- *raspberry tofu-based frozen dessert layered in parfait glasses with quartered kiwi slices*
- *scoops of pineapple sherbet or frozen yogurt ringed with whole raspberries*
- *orange sherbet topped with blueberries*
- *peach frozen yogurt with sliced peaches.*

Valley Girls' Sandwiches

HEALTH FOOD, CALIFORNIA STYLE

This is the ultimate West Coast sandwich, stuffed with vitamin-rich vegetables and mellow Monterey jack cheese—thick, tasty, nourishing, trendy and low in fat and calories. Serve it with a cold, creamy drink made of fresh bananas and yogurt.

Menu for 4

- **Frosty Banana Coolers**
- **Valley Girls' Sandwiches**
- **Fruit Rainbow**

SHOPPING LIST

- ☐ 1 6-ounce package sliced Monterey jack cheese
- ☐ 2 medium tomatoes
- ☐ 2 small cucumbers
- ☐ 1 pound fresh spinach
- ☐ 1 small package alfalfa sprouts
- ☐ 2 bananas
- ☐ 2 ripe peaches or nectarines
- ☐ 1 small bunch seedless purple grapes
- ☐ 1 pint strawberries or 1 10-ounce package frozen strawberries
- ☐ 1 kiwi fruit
- ☐ 1 loaf sliced dark pumpernickel or rye bread
- ☐ 1 small can or package chopped walnuts
- ☐ 1 8-ounce container low-fat vanilla yogurt
- ☐ 1 8-ounce container plain yogurt

Have on Hand
- ☐ Salt
- ☐ Pepper
- ☐ Low-fat milk
- ☐ Eggs
- ☐ Margarine

SCHEDULE

1. Mix Frosty Banana Coolers.
2. Prepare Valley Girls' Sandwiches.
3. Prepare Fruit Rainbow.

Frosty Banana Coolers

2   eggs
1   cup low-fat milk
1   container (8 oz.) low-fat
      vanilla yogurt
2   bananas

Place all ingredients in blender. Whirl to mix. Refrigerate until serving time.

Valley Girls' Sandwiches

2   small cucumbers, peeled
8   slices dark pumpernickel
       or rye bread
1½   tablespoons margarine,
       softened
8   slices (1 6-oz. package)
       Monterey jack cheese
2   medium tomatoes, very
       thinly sliced
4   tablespoons plain yogurt,
       divided
½   teaspoon salt
⅛   teaspoon pepper
1   cup alfalfa sprouts
16   spinach leaves

With vegetable peeler cut cucumbers into ⅛-inch lengthwise slices. Spread each slice of bread with about ½ teaspoon margarine. On each of 4 slices layer 1 slice cheese, 3 slices tomato, 1 teaspoon yogurt, salt and pepper to taste, 3 slices cucumber, ¼ cup alfalfa sprouts and 3 spinach leaves. Top with remaining bread.

Fruit Rainbow

1   kiwi fruit, peeled and
      sliced
1   pint strawberries or 1
      package (10 oz.) frozen
      strawberries, thawed
1   small bunch seedless
      purple grapes, halved
2   ripe peaches or nectarines,
      peeled, pitted and sliced
¼   cup chopped walnuts

Arrange 1 or 2 kiwi slices in center of each of 4 dessert dishes. Surround with rings of strawberries, grapes and peach or nectarine slices. Sprinkle chopped nuts over fruit.

THE BIG CHEESE

• *For calcium with less calories, try these cheeses: skim milk ricotta, Parmesan, cottage cheese with 1% milk fat, skim milk mozzarella, Jarlsberg and other Swiss-type cheese.*

Vitamin Burgers

BEEF PATTIES WITH VEGETABLE-FLAVORED SAUCE

Serve these hamburgers in a sauce made of vegetable juices and spiced with onion and red pepper sauce. Accompanied by a salad of fresh vegetables and hot or cool pita bread triangles, this makes a quick and tasty meal for summer or winter.

Menu for 4

- **Chilled Borscht**
- **Vitamin Burgers Cucumbers and Sliced Onions**
- **Whole Wheat Pita Triangles Fresh Pineapple Chunks**

SHOPPING LIST

- ☐ 2 medium onions
- ☐ 2 medium cucumbers
- ☐ 1 ripe pineapple
- ☐ 1 bunch fresh dill or dillweed
- ☐ 4 whole wheat pita breads
- ☐ 1 16-ounce can beets
- ☐ 1 12-ounce can cocktail vegetable juice
- ☐ 1 8-ounce container plain low-fat yogurt
- ☐ 1 pound ground beef

Have on Hand
- ☐ Salt
- ☐ Pepper
- ☐ Sugar
- ☐ Margarine

- ☐ 1 lemon or lemon juice
- ☐ Wheat germ
- ☐ Red pepper sauce
- ☐ Celery salt
- ☐ Oregano

SCHEDULE

1. Prepare Chilled Borscht.
2. Cut pineapple into chunks; cover and refrigerate.
3. Slice cucumbers and onions.
4. Cook Vegetable Burgers.
5. Prepare Whole Wheat Pita Triangles.

Chilled Borscht

1   tablespoon chopped onion
1   can (16 oz.) beets,
        undrained
1   container (8 oz.) plain
        low-fat yogurt
1   tablespoon chopped fresh
        dill or ½ teaspoon
        dillweed
1   teaspoon lemon juice
½   teaspoon salt
⅛   teaspoon pepper

In blender puree onion and beets with their liquid. Add yogurt, dill, lemon juice, salt and pepper. Cover and blend just until smooth. Chill in freezer for 20 minutes or longer. Stir before serving.

Vitamin Burgers

1   pound ground beef
1   cup cocktail vegetable
        juice, divided
2   tablespoons minced onion
¼   teaspoon salt
¼   teaspoon celery salt
4   drops red pepper sauce
1   teaspoon margarine
¼   teaspoon sugar
¼   teaspoon oregano

Mix ground beef, ¼ cup cocktail vegetable juice, onion, salt, celery salt and red pepper sauce; shape into 4 patties. In large skillet heat margarine; add beef patties and cook to desired doneness, 4 to 5 minutes on each side for medium. Re-

move and keep warm. In same skillet heat remaining ¾ cup cocktail vegetable juice, sugar and oregano until thick. Serve sauce over patties.

Whole Wheat Pita Triangles

4   whole wheat pita breads
2   teaspoons margarine
4   teaspoons wheat germ

Preheat broiler. Cut each pita bread into 6 wedges. Open each wedge and cut in half along crease to form 2 triangles. Spread a small amount of margarine on inside surface of each pita triangle; sprinkle with wheat germ. Arrange pita wedges crust side down on ungreased cookie sheet. Broil 3 to 5 minutes or until golden. Serve warm or at room temperature.

WHEAT GERM TIPS

• *For a quick party snack or family appetizer, stuff celery sticks with cottage cheese and sprinkle with wheat germ.*

• *Top sliced bananas with plain low-fat yogurt and 1 teaspoon wheat germ.*

• *Sprinkle liberally over cooked cereals.*

• *Mix equal parts wheat germ and margarine; spread over apple slices before baking.*

Chilled Szechuan Turkey

TURKEY WITH SOY-FLAVORED SAUCE

Soy sauce and sesame oil give this meal its Asian flavor. The high-fiber, low-calorie steamed-vegetable recipe works equally well with fresh broccoli when asparagus is unavailable. Look for rice crackers in Asian stores if your market doesn't carry them.

Menu for 4

- **Chilled Szechuan Turkey**
- **Oriental Asparagus**
- **Rice Crackers**

Orange Ice

SHOPPING LIST

☐	¾	pound sliced cooked turkey
☐	1½	pounds fresh asparagus
☐	1	bunch green onions
☐	1	head lettuce
☐	1	medium piece fresh ginger
☐	1	small jar sesame seed
☐	1	small bottle sesame oil
☐	1	package rice crackers
☐	1	pint orange ice

☐ Salad oil
☐ Soy sauce
☐ Red pepper sauce
☐ Honey

Have on Hand
☐ Garlic

SCHEDULE

1. Prepare sauce for turkey; chill.
2. Cook Oriental Asparagus.
3. Arrange Chilled Szechuan Turkey platter.

Chilled Szechuan Turkey

2	tablespoons soy sauce
1	tablespoon honey
1	small garlic clove, minced
1½	tablespoons salad oil
2	green onions, chopped
1	teaspoon minced fresh ginger
2	drops red pepper sauce
	Lettuce leaves
¾	pound sliced cooked turkey

In measuring cup combine soy sauce, honey and garlic; set aside. In small skillet heat oil over medium heat. Add remaining ingredients except lettuce leaves and turkey slices and saute 5 minutes. Turn off heat and add soy sauce mixture to skillet. Pour sauce into measuring cup or small bowl; chill in refrigerator 10 to 15 minutes. At serving time line salad platter with lettuce leaves. Arrange turkey slices on top; pour sauce over turkey.

Oriental Asparagus

1½	pounds fresh asparagus, trimmed
1	tablespoon salad oil
1½	teaspoons soy sauce
1	teaspoon sesame oil
1	teaspoon water
1	small garlic clove, pressed
1	slice fresh ginger
1	tablespoon toasted sesame seed

In large skillet or saucepan heat 1 inch water to boiling. Arrange asparagus in steamer basket and place over boiling water. Cover and steam 5 to 10 minutes or until tender-crisp. Remove from heat and cool. In small jar with tight-fitting lid combine salad oil, soy sauce, sesame oil, water, garlic and ginger; cover and shake. Pour over asparagus and turn to coat each spear. Marinate at room temperature or in refrigerator until serving time. Remove ginger slice and sprinkle sesame seed over asparagus spears.

HOW TO USE FRESH GINGER

- *Fresh ginger is a root, knobby and irregular in shape. Buy only a small chunk; a little goes a long way. With sharp knife, cut a thin slice out of the fat section of a knob. Trim off and discard the skin. Use 1 or 2 of these slices to flavor a dish; remove them before serving.*
- *Or mince the ginger very finely and add to the dish before cooking.*
- *Fresh ginger will give stronger flavor to foods than ground ginger.*
- *To store, wrap tightly in plastic or place cut side down in dry sherry in covered plastic dish. Refrigerate.*

Ginger Beef

FLANK STEAK WITH SOY AND FRESH GINGER

There is almost no limit to the number and variety of quick, healthful stir-fry combinations you can serve. This one makes use of tender flank steak, onions, ginger and garlic. The lemon-flavored carrots and snow peas provide a tangy complement to the entree.

═══ Menu for 4 ═══

- **Ginger Beef**
  Rice
- **Lemony Carrots and Snow Peas**
- **Broiled Peaches**

SHOPPING LIST

- ☐ ¾ pound flank steak
- ☐ 1 medium onion
- ☐ 1 small piece fresh ginger
- ☐ 1 pound carrots
- ☐ ¼ pound snow peas
- ☐ 1 lemon
- ☐ 4 peaches
- ☐ 1 13¾- or 14½-ounce can beef broth
- ☐ 1 package almond cookies

Have on Hand

- ☐ Cornstarch
- ☐ Brown sugar
- ☐ Salt
- ☐ Margarine

- ☐ Long-grain rice
- ☐ Garlic
- ☐ Salad oil
- ☐ Soy sauce
- ☐ Crushed red pepper
- ☐ Fruit-flavored liqueur (optional)

SCHEDULE

1. Cook rice.
2. Prepare Lemony Carrots and Snow Peas.
3. Prepare Ginger Beef.
4. Prepare Broiled Peaches.

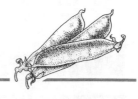

Ginger Beef

1   tablespoon cornstarch
¼   cup beef broth
3   tablespoons soy sauce
1   teaspoon salad oil
1   medium onion, sliced
¾   pound flank steak, cut on
        the diagonal into thin strips
1   teaspoon minced fresh ginger
1   garlic clove, crushed
    Dash crushed red pepper

In small bowl combine cornstarch, broth and soy sauce; stir and set aside.

In wok or large skillet heat oil; add onion and stir-fry 1 minute. Stir in steak, ginger and garlic; stir-fry 3 to 5 minutes more, until meat is browned. Add broth mixture and red pepper; stir-fry another 2 minutes. Serve immediately.

Lemony Carrots and Snow Peas

1   pound carrots, peeled and
        cut into ¼-inch slices
¼   pound snow peas, trimmed
2   tablespoons margarine
1   tablespoon lemon juice
1   teaspoon lemon peel

In medium saucepan cook carrots in boiling salted water to cover about 10 minutes, until tender; drain well. In separate saucepan cook snow peas in boiling water to cover about 6 minutes, until tender; drain well.

In large skillet or wok melt margarine over medium heat until bubbly; add lemon juice and peel; stir to mix. Add carrots and snow peas to skillet and stir-fry until coated and heated through.

Broiled Peaches

4   peaches, peeled, pitted and
        halved
2   tablespoons margarine
1   tablespoon brown sugar
4   teaspoons fruit-flavored
        liqueur (optional)

Preheat broiler. Arrange peach halves, cut side up, on greased baking sheet. Dot with margarine and sprinkle lightly with brown sugar. Broil 8 to 10 minutes until sizzling but not mushy.

SHORT COURSE IN CARROT CUTTING

- To Dice: *Cut carrot into equal strips lengthwise. Stack and slice again in lengthwise strips; cut strips crosswise into cubes.*
- To Slice: *Place carrot on flattest side. Cut crosswise into slices of uniform thickness.*
- To Julienne: *Slice carrot into 3-inch lengths. Then cut into strips. Stack; cut same way into thinner strips.*

Watercress Burgers

TERIYAKI PATTIES WITH SPROUT SALAD

A change from the usual burger fare, these beef patties get their unique flavor from ginger, watercress and teriyaki sauce. Add a tahini-rich sprout salad and finish the meal with ambrosia prepared in the traditional manner.

Menu for 4

- **Watercress Burgers**
- **Korean Sprout Salad**
- **Cellophane Noodles or Thin Egg Noodles**
- **Classic Ambrosia**

SHOPPING LIST

- ☐ 5 ounces bean sprouts
- ☐ 1 red pepper
- ☐ 1 bunch green onions
- ☐ 1 bunch radishes
- ☐ 1 head Chinese cabbage
- ☐ 1 bunch watercress
- ☐ 3 oranges
- ☐ 1 coconut or 1 small can or package shredded coconut
- ☐ 1 small can or package blanched almonds
- ☐ 1 package cellophane noodles or thin egg noodles
- ☐ 1 small jar tahini (sesame paste)
- ☐ 1 small jar sesame seed
- ☐ 1 small bottle teriyaki sauce
- ☐ 1 pound ground beef

Have on Hand

- ☐ Sugar
- ☐ Salt
- ☐ Pepper
- ☐ Garlic
- ☐ Salad oil
- ☐ Red wine vinegar
- ☐ Soy sauce
- ☐ Ground ginger
- ☐ Bread (for bread crumbs)

SCHEDULE

1. Prepare Classic Ambrosia.
2. Prepare salad and dressing.
3. Cook noodles.
4. Prepare Watercress Burgers.
5. Toss Korean Sprout Salad.

Watercress Burgers

1   pound ground beef
1/4 teaspoon ground ginger
1/8 teaspoon salt
1/8 teaspoon pepper
3/4 cup coarsely chopped
     watercress
1   garlic clove, pressed
1/2 cup fresh bread crumbs
3   tablespoons water, divided
1   tablespoon salad oil
3   tablespoons teriyaki sauce

In large bowl combine ground beef with ginger, salt, pepper, watercress, garlic, bread crumbs and 2 tablespoons water. Shape into 4 patties. In large skillet heat oil. Add burgers and cook until browned, about 5 minutes on each side. Transfer to serving platter.

Wipe out skillet; add teriyaki sauce and 1 tablespoon water; heat. Pour over patties and serve immediately.

Korean Sprout Salad

2   tablespoons salad oil
1   tablespoon red wine
     vinegar
1   tablespoon soy sauce
1   small garlic clove
1   tablespoon tahini (sesame
     seed paste)
1/2 teaspoon sugar
     Dash salt
2   cups (about 5 oz.) bean sprouts

1/2 cup chopped red pepper
1/4 cup chopped green onions
3   radishes, julienned
1/2 cup shredded Chinese
     cabbage
1   tablespoon toasted sesame
     seed

In blender combine first seven ingredients for dressing; cover and blend on high speed until smooth, about 30 seconds. Set aside. Just before serving, combine vegetables in large bowl; pour on dressing and toss. Sprinkle sesame seed on top.

Classic Ambrosia

2   cups sliced oranges, with
     juice
1/2 cup shredded coconut,
     fresh if possible
1/3 cup chopped blanched
     almonds

Place orange slices in medium bowl. Sprinkle with coconut and almonds and chill well.

CELLOPHANE NOODLES

These transparent treats are not really noodles at all—they're a vegetable product made from the mung bean. Use them alone or in soups and stir-fried dishes. To prepare: Soak the noodles in warm water until they soften, about 10 minutes; drain, cut into shorter lengths and cook 5 minutes in simmering water or broth.

Liver Braised in Tomato Sauce

IRON-RICH ENTREE WITH BULGUR WHEAT

Nutrients abound in this hearty and satisfying dinner. A refreshing and tasty change from the usual liver and onions, this entree is braised in savory cumin-flavored tomatoes. The luscious dessert is sure to become a standby for family and company meals.

Menu for 4

- **Liver Braised in Tomato Sauce with Cumin Bulgur**
- **Steamed Zucchini**
- **Berries with Banana Cream**

SHOPPING LIST

- ☐ 1 pound sliced beef liver
- ☐ 1 bunch green onions
- ☐ 3 medium zucchini
- ☐ 1 pint strawberries or raspberries
- ☐ 1 medium very ripe banana
- ☐ 1 package bulgur (cracked wheat)
- ☐ 1 13¾- or 14½-ounce can beef broth
- ☐ 1 16-ounce can crushed tomatoes
- ☐ 1 small jar chopped pimientos
- ☐ 1 8-ounce container plain low-fat yogurt

Have on Hand
- ☐ All-purpose flour

- ☐ Sugar
- ☐ Salt
- ☐ Pepper
- ☐ Garlic
- ☐ Milk
- ☐ Honey
- ☐ Salad oil
- ☐ Cumin

SCHEDULE

1. Prepare Berries and Banana Cream; refrigerate separately.
2. Cook bulgur.
3. Cook Liver Braised in Tomato Sauce with Cumin.
4. Prepare Steamed Zucchini.

Liver Braised in Tomato Sauce with Cumin

1   *pound sliced beef liver*
    Milk
1/3 *cup all-purpose flour*
1/8 *teaspoon salt*
    Dash pepper
3   *tablespoons salad oil*
1   *teaspoon cumin*
1   *garlic clove, pressed*
1   *can (16 oz.) crushed tomatoes,*
      undrained
1/2 *cup beef broth*
1/4 *cup sliced green onions,*
      divided
1/4 *teaspoon sugar*

In shallow dish combine liver and just enough milk to cover. Set aside at room temperature 5 to 10 minutes. In another shallow dish combine flour, salt and pepper. Drain liver and dip both sides into flour, shaking off excess.

In 12-inch skillet heat oil. Add liver; brown quickly on both sides. Transfer to platter. To drippings in skillet add cumin and garlic; saute 1 minute. Add remaining ingredients except 1 tablespoon onion and liver; cook 5 minutes. Add liver; simmer 3 to 5 minutes. Garnish with remaining onion.

Steamed Zucchini

3   *medium zucchini*
2   *tablespoons chopped onion*
4   *tablespoons chopped pimiento*

Freshly ground pepper

Trim ends from zucchini and cut into 1/4-inch slices. In large saucepan or steamer bring 1 inch water to a boil. Place zucchini slices and chopped onion in steamer basket and set in boiling water. Cover and steam about 5 minutes, until tender but not limp. Transfer to serving bowl and toss with chopped pimiento and pepper.

Berries with Banana Cream

1   *pint fresh strawberries or*
      raspberries
1/2 *cup plain low-fat yogurt*
1   *medium very ripe banana,*
      sliced
1   *teaspoon honey*

Wash and trim berries. Set aside 1/2 cup berries, sliced or quartered if very large. Place remaining berries in 4 dessert dishes; refrigerate. In blender combine reserved berries with remaining ingredients; cover and blend until smooth. Spoon on top of berries at serving time.

BERRY TIPS

- *Whenever possible, buy local berries rather than berries grown far away and picked while green, which are not as juicy and tasty.*
- *If you can, lift up the top berries and check the ones underneath to make sure they're not bruised or overripe.*

Scallops Provençal

CONTINENTAL SEAFOOD MENU

Fresh sea scallops gently simmered with tomatoes and mushrooms add up to simplicity and elegance for a family or company dinner. Add linguine, a tarragon-flavored tossed salad and lime-and-wine-spiked poached pears for a meal to serve with pride.

=== **Menu for 4** ===

- **Scallops Provençal Linguine**
- **Tossed Salad with Tarragon Dressing**
- **Poached Pears**

SHOPPING LIST

- ☐ 1 pound sea scallops
- ☐ ½ pound mushrooms
- ☐ 1 bunch green onions
- ☐ 2 large tomatoes
- ☐ 1 medium head romaine lettuce
- ☐ 1 green pepper
- ☐ 1 small cucumber
- ☐ 1 bunch fresh parsley
- ☐ 4 ripe pears
- ☐ 1 lime
- ☐ 1 package linguine
- ☐ 1 8-ounce container plain low-fat yogurt
- ☐ Sauternes

Have on Hand
- ☐ Sugar

- ☐ Salt
- ☐ Pepper
- ☐ Garlic
- ☐ Olive oil
- ☐ 1 lemon or lemon juice
- ☐ Dijon mustard
- ☐ Oregano
- ☐ Tarragon

SCHEDULE

1. Prepare Poached Pears.
2. Prepare salad greens and dressing.
3. Cook linguine.
4. Prepare Scallops Provençal.

Scallops Provençal

1   pound sea scallops, cut in half
3   tablespoons lemon juice
½   pound mushrooms, sliced
½   cup sliced green onions
      with tops
2   tablespoons olive oil, divided
2   tablespoons chopped fresh
      parsley
½   teaspoon oregano
2   large tomatoes, peeled and
      coarsely chopped, or 1½
      cups canned tomatoes,
      drained and chopped
      Parsley sprigs

In small bowl marinate scallops in lemon juice; set aside. In medium skillet saute mushrooms and green onions in 1 tablespoon oil until golden. Add chopped parsley, oregano and tomatoes. Simmer gently for 5 minutes and set aside. In large skillet saute scallops in remaining 1 tablespoon oil until golden and cooked through, 3 to 5 minutes. Combine scallops with sauce; garnish with parsley sprigs.

Tossed Salad with Tarragon Dressing

1   medium head romaine
      lettuce, torn into bite-
      size pieces
1   green pepper, cut into chunks
1   small cucumber, sliced
½   cup plain low-fat yogurt
1½ teaspoons Dijon mustard
½   teaspoon tarragon
      Dash pepper
      Dash sugar

In salad bowl combine lettuce, pepper and cucumber. In measuring cup combine remaining ingredients; stir well to mix. Toss with salad at serving time.

Poached Pears

3   cups sauternes
4   ripe pears, peeled, cored
      and halved
3   tablespoons sugar or to
      taste
      Juice of 1 lime

In large saucepan bring sauterne just to a boil. Add pears and simmer until tender, about 20 minutes, adding sugar as necessary. Transfer pears and liquid to medium bowl. Stir in lime juice and refrigerate until serving time.

PROVENÇAL DISHES

The term "Provençal" usually designates foods cooked with tomatoes and garlic. Try simmering, poaching or braising these foods in the Provençal style using fresh garlic (always) and fresh or canned tomatoes:
* *zucchini*
* *white fish fillets or steaks*
* *chicken cutlets*
* *sliced eggplant*
* *flank or round steak*
* *artichokes*

Crunchy Tuna Salad

BULGUR, TUNA, TOMATOES, and GREEN ONIONS

This main-dish salad gets its crunch from cracked wheat and zucchini. With this low-calorie, high-fiber entree serve a vegetable medley of cauliflower, snow peas and cherry tomatoes with the cool flavor of fresh dill and lime juice.

Menu for 4

- **Crunchy Tuna Salad**
- **Vegetables with Lime-Dill Dressing**

Melba Toast
Berry-Flavored Frozen Tofu-Based Dessert

SHOPPING LIST

- ☐ 1   6½- or 7-ounce can water-packed tuna
- ☐ 1   bunch green onions
- ☐ 1   pint cherry tomatoes
- ☐ 1   medium zucchini
- ☐ 1   head lettuce
- ☐ 1   small cauliflower
- ☐ ¼   pound snow peas
- ☐ 1   bunch watercress
- ☐ 1   bunch fresh mint
- ☐ 1   bunch fresh dill
- ☐ 1   lime or lime juice
- ☐ 1   small package bulgur wheat
- ☐ 1   package Melba toast
- ☐ 1   8-ounce container plain low-fat yogurt
- ☐ 1   pint berry-flavored frozen tofu-based dessert

Have on Hand

- ☐   Sugar
- ☐   Pepper
- ☐   Salad oil
- ☐   Dijon mustard

SCHEDULE

1. Soak bulgur.
2. Prepare Vegetables with Lime-Dill Dressing.
3. Prepare Crunchy Tuna Salad.

Crunchy Tuna Salad

¼ *cup bulgur (cracked wheat)*
½ *cup hot water*
½ *cup plain low-fat yogurt*
2 *tablespoons chopped mint*
1 *tablespoon Dijon mustard*
2 *tablespoons thinly sliced green onion*
1 *can (6½ or 7 oz.) water-packed tuna, drained*
1 *cup diced zucchini Lettuce leaves*

In medium bowl combine bulgur and water. Let stand 25 minutes. Drain off and discard excess water. Stir yogurt, mint, mustard and green onion into bulgur. Add tuna and zucchini, stirring gently to break up tuna and coat with yogurt mixture. Line small plates with lettuce leaves and top with tuna mixture.

Vegetables with Lime-Dill Dressing

2 *cups cauliflower florets*
1 *cup snow peas*
1 *pint cherry tomatoes*
½ *cup watercress, cut into pieces*
2 *tablespoons lime juice*
1 *tablespoon salad oil*
2 *teaspoons chopped fresh dill*
½ *teaspoon sugar Dash pepper*

In medium saucepan blanch cauliflower in boiling water to cover for 10 seconds. Drain and cool in cold water; set aside. Blanch snow peas in boiling water 10 seconds; drain and cool. In large bowl toss snow peas with cauliflower; add cherry tomatoes and watercress.

In measuring cup combine remaining ingredients; stir to blend well. Pour over vegetables and toss to coat. Let stand at room temperature until serving time; toss again.

APPETIZER VEGETABLE DIP

As a first course or a party snack serve cold blanched cauliflower florets and snow peas with a dip made from:

1 cup plain low-fat yogurt
⅓ cup chopped green onions
1 tablespoon chopped fresh dill
1 teaspoon Worcestershire sauce
¼ teaspoon salt
⅛ teaspoon seasoned pepper

Stir all ingredients together in medium bowl until blended.

Flounder Fillets in Foil

LOW-FAT, LOW-CALORIE SEAFOOD DINNER

When flounder is unavailable, use other fresh white fillets to make this foil-baked fish dinner. Serve the creamy summer squash soup hot or place it in the freezer for a while and serve it chilled, garnished with fresh dill sprigs.

Menu for 4

- **Yellow Squash Soup**
- **Flounder Fillets in Foil**

Rice
- **Dilled Green Beans**

Lemon Sherbet

SHOPPING LIST

- ☐ 4 flounder fillets
- ☐ 1 pound green beans
- ☐ 2 medium yellow summer squash
- ☐ 2 medium onions
- ☐ ½ pound mushrooms
- ☐ 1 green pepper
- ☐ 1 large or 2 small shallots or 1 bunch green onions
- ☐ 1 bunch fresh dill or dillweed
- ☐ 1 bunch fresh parsley or parsley flakes
- ☐ 2 13¾- or 14½-ounce cans chicken broth
- ☐ 1 13¾- or 14½-ounce can beef broth

- ☐ 1 8-ounce container plain low-fat yogurt
- ☐ 1 pint lemon sherbet

Have on Hand
- ☐ Long-grain rice
- ☐ Pepper
- ☐ 1 lemon or lemon juice
- ☐ Margarine or salad oil
- ☐ Dry white wine

SCHEDULE

1. Prepare Flounder Fillets in Foil.
2. Cook rice.
3. Prepare Yellow Squash Soup.
4. Prepare Dilled Green Beans.

Yellow Squash Soup

2 **medium yellow summer squash, sliced**
2 **medium onions, sliced**
2 **cans (13¾ or 14½ oz. each) chicken broth**
⅛ **teaspoon pepper**
¼ **cup plain low-fat yogurt**

In medium saucepan combine squash, onions and chicken broth; bring to a boil and simmer 15 minutes, or until vegetables are soft. Add pepper and yogurt. Puree soup in blender. Add more yogurt and pepper if you wish.

Flounder Fillets in Foil

2 **tablespoons margarine, divided**
2 **tablespoons chopped shallots or green onions**
½ **pound mushrooms, chopped**
3 **tablespoons dry white wine**
1 **tablespoon lemon juice**
1 **tablespoon chopped parsley**
4 **flounder fillets**
⅛ **teaspoon pepper**

In medium skillet melt 1 tablespoon margarine and saute shallots or green onions until soft. Add mushrooms and cook 5 minutes. Stir in wine, lemon juice and parsley. Cook until most of liquid has evaporated.

Preheat oven to 400° F. Lightly grease 4 sheets of heavy-duty foil with margarine or oil. Place a fillet on each sheet; season with pepper. Spoon some mushroom sauce over each fillet. Draw edges of foil together and seal. Bake for 20 minutes or until fish flakes when tested with a fork.

Dilled Green Beans

2 **tablespoons chopped onion**
¼ **cup chopped green pepper**
1 **teaspoon fresh dill or ½ teaspoon dillweed**
1 **can (13¾ or 14½ oz.) beef broth**
2 **cups water**
1 **pound fresh green beans, trimmed**

In large saucepan combine onion, pepper, dill, broth and water. Bring to a boil; cook over medium heat 5 minutes. Add beans and return liquid to a boil. Lower heat to medium, cover, and cook 8 to 10 minutes, until beans are tender-crisp.

MUSHROOM TIPS

- *In 1¼ cups of mushrooms there are only 29 calories, so use these vegetables lavishly.*
- *Never soak them. Wipe them clean with a damp cloth or run briefly under cold water just before cooking. Pat dry.*
- *Do not peel mushrooms; the almost invisible skin contains important nutrients.*
- *Use stems as well as caps, but slice away the ends if they're tough.*

Spicy Skewered Shrimp

BROILED SHRIMP WITH A BLENDER SOUP

Here is a company-special seafood dinner suitable for entertaining on the patio, but simple and light enough for hurry-up family meals as well.

Menu for 4

- **Watercress Soup**
- **Spicy Skewered Shrimp**

- **Refreshing Zucchini Salad**
- **Whole Wheat Rolls**

Chilled Seedless Grapes

SHOPPING LIST

- ☐ 1½ pounds medium shrimp
- ☐ 2 medium zucchini
- ☐ 1 bunch green onions
- ☐ 1 bunch watercress
- ☐ 1 small white onion
- ☐ 1 bunch seedless grapes
- ☐ 2 lemons or lemon juice
- ☐ 1 package whole wheat rolls
- ☐ 1 13¾- or 14½-ounce can chicken broth
- ☐ 1 8-ounce container plain low-fat yogurt

Have on Hand
- ☐ Sugar
- ☐ Salt
- ☐ Low-fat milk
- ☐ Eggs

- ☐ Margarine
- ☐ Garlic
- ☐ Olive oil
- ☐ Honey
- ☐ Chili sauce
- ☐ Red pepper sauce
- ☐ Oregano
- ☐ Nutmeg

SCHEDULE

1. Marinate shrimp.
2. Prepare Refreshing Zucchini Salad.
3. Prepare Watercress Soup.
4. Broil Spicy Skewered Shrimp.

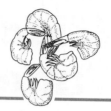

Watercress Soup

1   bunch watercress, washed
1   cup chicken broth
1   small white onion, peeled
      and quartered
1   small garlic clove, peeled
      and halved
1   egg yolk
1   cup low-fat milk
2   tablespoons margarine,
      melted
1   teaspoon sugar
1   teaspoon nutmeg
½   teaspoon salt

Combine all ingredients in blender. Blend for 1 minute or until smooth. Pour mixture into saucepan and heat slowly until piping hot, stirring occasionally.

Spicy Skewered Shrimp

1½   pounds medium shrimp,
        shelled and deveined
3   tablespoons olive oil
¼   cup chili sauce
1   teaspoon salt
1   teaspoon oregano
½   teaspoon red pepper sauce
2   garlic cloves, crushed
3   tablespoons lemon juice

Shell and devein shrimp but leave tail shells attached. In large bowl mix shrimp with remaining ingredients and turn to coat. Marinate at room temperature 15 minutes.

Preheat broiler or prepare grill. Drain shrimp thoroughly, thread them on metal skewers and broil 4 to 5 inches from heat for 5 minutes on each side.

Refreshing Zucchini Salad

4   tablespoons plain low-fat
        yogurt
1½   teaspoons lemon juice
½   teaspoon honey
½   teaspoon oregano, crushed
¼   teaspoon salt
2   cups thinly sliced
        zucchini
½   cup coarsely chopped
        green onions

In large bowl combine yogurt, lemon juice, honey, oregano and salt; mix well. Stir in zucchini and green onions; toss to coat. Chill until serving time.

SHRIMP TIPS

- *Shrimp is versatile, high in nutrients and taste, quick and easy to prepare and almost universally popular.*
- *Toss cooked, shelled shrimp with chilled grapefruit sections and a little vinaigrette dressing; serve in grapefruit shells as appetizer.*
- *Serve with asparagus spears and lemon wedges as luncheon entree.*
- *Present on lettuce leaves with ketchup-horseradish sauce—the classic shrimp cocktail.*

Middle Eastern Turkeyburgers

TURKEY PATTIES, LENTILS AND A TOSSED SALAD

Ground turkey is lower in fat than ground beef and makes a refreshing change from hamburgers. Serve the Gingered Lentils hot or at room temperature and avoid overcooking them; they should not be mushy.

Menu for 4

- **Middle Eastern Turkeyburgers**
- **Gingered Lentils**
- **Tossed Salad with Healthy Vinaigrette**
- **Grapes**

SHOPPING LIST

- ☐ 1 pound ground turkey
- ☐ 1 bunch green onions
- ☐ 1 green pepper
- ☐ 1 head lettuce
- ☐ 1 large tomato or 1 pint cherry tomatoes
- ☐ 1 small cucumber
- ☐ 1 small piece fresh ginger
- ☐ 1 bunch fresh chives
- ☐ 1 large bunch grapes
- ☐ 1 lemon
- ☐ 1 small package lentils
- ☐ 1 8-ounce container plain low-fat yogurt
- ☐ 4 pita breads

Have on Hand
- ☐ Salt

- ☐ Pepper
- ☐ Garlic
- ☐ Salad oil
- ☐ Cider vinegar
- ☐ White wine vinegar
- ☐ Curry powder or cumin
- ☐ Capers
- ☐ Dry mustard
- ☐ Paprika

SCHEDULE

1. Cook Gingered Lentils.
2. Prepare salad and dressing.
3. Cook Middle Eastern Turkeyburgers.

Middle Eastern Turkeyburgers

1 *pound raw ground turkey*
½ *cup chopped green onions, divided*
1 *garlic clove, minced*
½ *teaspoon grated lemon peel*
½ *teaspoon curry powder or ¼ teaspoon cumin*
¼ *teaspoon pepper*
½ *cup plain low-fat yogurt*
4 *pita breads, warmed*

Prepare charcoal grill or preheat broiler. In medium bowl combine turkey, ¼ cup green onions, garlic, lemon peel, curry or cumin and pepper; blend well. Shape turkey mixture into 4 round patties. Grill or broil to desired doneness, about 5 minutes on each side for medium.

Meanwhile, in small bowl combine yogurt with remaining green onions. Serve burgers in pita breads topped with yogurt mixture.

Gingered Lentils

3 *cups water*
1 *cup lentils*
½ *teaspoon salt*
3 *tablespoons salad oil*
1 *teaspoon grated fresh ginger*
⅓ *cup chopped green onions*
⅓ *cup chopped green pepper*
2 *tablespoons white wine vinegar*

In medium saucepan heat water, lentils and salt to boiling. Reduce heat to me-

dium-low; cover and simmer 20 minutes, until lentils are tender but not mushy; drain lentils and set aside. In medium skillet heat oil and ginger for 1 minute, stirring often. Add green onions and pepper; stir-fry for 2 minutes. Stir in lentils and vinegar and cook until lentils are heated through.

Tossed Salad with Healthy Vinaigrette

1 *head lettuce, torn into bite-size pieces*
1 *large tomato, chopped, or 8 cherry tomatoes, halved*
1 *small cucumber, sliced*
1 *tablespoon plus 1 teaspoon salad oil*
2 *teaspoons water*
1 *tablespoon cider vinegar*
1 *teaspoon chopped fresh chives*
1 *teaspoon capers*
¼ *teaspoon paprika*
⅛ *teaspoon dry mustard*

In salad bowl combine lettuce, tomato and cucumber. In small jar with tight-fitting lid combine remaining ingredients and shake well to blend. Toss salad with dressing at serving time.

QUICK PROTEIN WITH LENTILS

High in fiber, low in fat and packed with vitamins, lentils provide more protein than any other vegetable.

Index

For information on how to subscribe to
Ladies' Home Journal, please write to:

Ladies' Home Journal
Box 10895
Des Moines, IA 50336-0895